WHAT JESUS MEANT

WHAT JESUS MEANT

THE BEATITUDES AND A
MEANINGFUL LIFE

Erik Kolbell

Westminster John Knox Press
LOUISVILLE • LONDON

Scripture quotations from the New Revised Standard Version of the Bible are copyright © 1989 by the Division of Christian Education of the National Council of the Churches of Christ in the U.S.A. and are used by permission.

Lyric from "Brokedown Palace" copyright Ice Nine Publishing Company. Used with permission.

Book design by Sharon Adams
Cover design by Mark Abrams

First edition
Published by Westminster John Knox Press
Louisville, Kentucky

This book is printed on acid-free paper that meets the American National Standards Institute Z39.48 standard. ♾

PRINTED IN THE UNITED STATES OF AMERICA

03 04 05 06 07 08 09 10 11 12 — 10 9 8 7 6 5 4 3 2 1

Library of Congress Cataloging-in-Publication Data

Kolbell, Erik.
      What Jesus meant : the Beatitudes and a meaningful life / Erik
Kolbell. — 1st ed.
            p. cm.
      ISBN 0-664-22292-7 (alk. paper)
      1. Beatitudes.   I. Title.

BT382 .K65 2003
241.5'3—dc21

                                                            2002033112

To my wife, Ann, and our daughter, Kate . . .
for their extravagant love

A religious person is a person who holds God and humanity in one thought at one time, at all times, who suffers harm done to others, whose greatest passion is compassion, whose greatest strength is love and defiance of despair.
—Abraham Heschel

The essential conditions of everything you do must be choice, love, passion.
—Nadia Boulanger

Contents

Foreword

I once heard an atheist psychiatrist say that there are more psychological insights in the Bible than in all the collected works of Freud. As if to support his contention, along comes this first-rate book on Jesus' Beatitudes written by a man who is both a psychotherapist and a Christian minister.

Why would he choose this subject at this time? Two reasons come to mind. For one, the Beatitudes are creed-free, nondoctrinal, more Jewish than anything else, but full of wisdom for believers of many faiths in this increasingly multifaith nation. The Beatitudes are also for people of no professed faith, at least for those who feel there must be more to life than what they are presently living, who wonder why this nation, so prosperous to so many, is so far from the promised land of our longing, and who are fearful that the world is on the brink of destruction.

A second reason recalls the well-known story about Gandhi, who one day was asked what he thought of Western civilization. He answered, "I think it would be a good idea." Something similar could be said today of Jesus' Beatitudes, because clearly they have little place among acceptable ideas in American culture.

Yet if we read and ponder these eight Beatitudes, especially with the imaginative commentary of Erik Kolbell, we will find that the result is similar to the conclusion of a good "whodunit": the surprise is the discovery of inevitability. Of course I'm personally unhappy; affluence, after all, can't buy morale. Of course the world's a mess; war is a coward's escape from the problems of peace.

In short, the Beatitudes challenge today's habitual expectations. They shake up our usual criteria of normalcy by presenting a new view of reality. While sounding peaceful enough, they are at heart profound and passionate, full of insights and authority for those of us prepared, in these precarious times, to reevaluate matters at the very core of our individual and collective lives.

Years ago, while still in seminary, I used to wonder what Jesus meant when he said, "Do not think that I have come to bring peace on earth; I have not come to bring peace, but a sword." Finally, I concluded that the sword Jesus must have had in mind was the sword of truth, the only sword that heals the wounds it inflicts.

Hurting and healing, each of Jesus' eight beatitudes is just such a sword. I felt it anew reading this beautiful book.

William Sloane Coffin

Preface

Anyone who thought it was Jesus' intent to found a new religion need look no further than the Beatitudes to realize he was merely trying to remind his followers of the brilliance of an old one. Each verse is drawn from the sacred writings of ancient Judaism. The Beatitudes—and the Sermon on the Mount that follows—are an exquisite expression of the promise and expectation of Judaism as first preached by the prophets of old.

In delivering these words Jesus is doing what every good rabbi has ever done for a lost and anxious congregation: he is taking them back to their roots. Their religion may have become compromised over the years, as does every institution forged by human hands. But their faith is a thing of eternal wisdom and incorruptible truth, and of this they needed reminding.

Many of us could have found ourselves on that mount that day, so hungry we are for the assuredness of faith if not the constraints of religion. We want to draw closer to God even if—over the years—we have drawn farther away from the church or synagogue of our birth. We want God to speak to us in ways that help us make sense of an increasingly sophisticated, secularized, fast-paced, and isolating world. We want to live more peacefully with ourselves, our families, and our neighbors. We want to alleviate the suffering of complete strangers as if they were our brothers or our sisters. We want warring nations to lay down their arms. We want sacred texts to bring the lessons of the past to the crises of the present. We want them to speak to us of how to instill good and noble values in our children and how to keep love alive in our marriages. We want them to help us find our moral compass in a world where equivocation is the refuge of cowards. We want to find a purpose to our lives that is greater than the sum total of our worldly possessions, our job title, or our social standing. We want a sense of permanence in a sea of change.

On more than one occasion in my life I've felt disappointed by Western religion's waning power to promote good in the world. I've been outraged by its inability to cure the senseless acts of violence inflicted by one human being upon another, and disturbed by the suffering of innocent children. I've also been chastened by my own eagerness to pursue the things that satisfy my ego at the expense of those that enrich my soul. On such occasions I have returned to these words again and again, always asking that they direct me to a clearer understanding of what it means to be a child of God in an era of such complexity and uncertainty. They have never been silent, and it would be my pleasure to extend to others some of the whispers that have wended their way from ear to heart.

These are wondrous verses. Each being derived from an ancient Hebrew text, we are assured in no uncertain terms that Jews and Christians are called to hew the same codes of conduct. I've long felt uneasy about people who exalt their own convictions by belittling someone else's, and at a time when respect for others is increasingly drowned out by the vice of intolerance disguised as the virtue of principle, my unease has only grown more pointed over the years. The burning of houses of worship, the bombing of clinics, the shooting of children by children, the baiting of races, the villification of immigrants, the gating of neighborhoods, all lead me to wonder if it is in our nature to always divide ourselves against ourselves. But when I sit awhile with the Beatitudes, I am taking a tonic for what ails my soul; their restorative powers remind me that not only does God speak a universal language of unconditional love, he expects us to do no less.

They are also wondrous because each is a poetic and exquisitely paradoxical meditation on how to live a life of faith in a world of doubt. In lilting beauty and fluid verse, the Beatitudes sanctify those qualities in us that are the very antithesis of success as we in the West have come to understand (and pursue) it. Their eight pillars—meekness, empathy, righteousness, peace, persecution, purity, poverty, and simplicity—are worthy things here, things to be dearly cherished and boldly lived. So when we find ourselves caught up in cravings for status or station, when we're itching to be rewarded for something we've done, the Beatitudes take those cravings and flip them on their head, as if to say, "If you want to live a life of faith, aspire to that which you disdain and disdain that to which you aspire."

They are also wondrous because each one binds the personal promise of faith to the public imperative of discipleship. When Jesus blesses the "poor in spirit," he's instructing us to examine our own desires for physical comforts—the new car, or fancier computer, or bigger home. He's asking us if those desires compromise both our allegiance to God *and* our responsibility to the legions of homeless, hopeless, jobless, and friendless people we encounter every day on the hard streets of our cities and towns. In the blessedness of those who "hunger and thirst for righteousness" there can be heard both an invitation to cleanse our souls through the ancient rite of fasting and a plea to entire nations to exercise greater discipline in their use of our world's increasingly scarce natural resources.

Finally, they are wondrous because they're accessible, because we can read them as though Jesus himself has sifted through the great thicket of ancient wisdom and laid bare its very essence before our eyes. Eight pillars of extravagant wisdom: Though they are of few words, we will not find one single statute, law, commandment, proverb, parable, or homily in all the Bible that is not in some way reflected in one of these verses that the Rabbi has lifted up before us.

And he opened his mouth, and taught them, saying:
Blessed are the poor in spirit,
for theirs is the kingdom of heaven.
Blessed are those who mourn, for they shall be comforted.
Blessed are the meek, for they shall inherit the earth.
Blessed are those who hunger and thirst for righteousness,
for they shall be satisfied.
Blessed are the merciful, for they shall obtain mercy.
Blessed are the pure in heart, for they shall see God.
Blessed are the peacemakers, for they shall be called
children of God.
Blessed are those who are persecuted for righteousness' sake,
for theirs is the kingdom of heaven.

(Matt. 5:2–10)

1

The Rabbi Shows Us the Way
of the Kingdom

> *The character which we find in the Beatitudes is, beyond
> all question, nothing less than our Lord's own character,
> put into words. It is the description set side by side with an
> example.*
>
> —Billy Graham, *The Secret of Happiness*

*T*hough Jesus spent at least three years of his life (around 24 to 27
of the Common Era) preaching to audiences both great and small,
precious few of his words have been filtered down to us in reliable
fashion. Fortunately though, what we *do* have, in the fifth chapter
of the Gospel According to Matthew (and, in a slightly different
version, in Luke), is what scholars believe to be as concise, precise, and thorough a collection of his teaching as we are ever likely
to find.

In what came to be called the Sermon on the Mount, the intro-
duction to which is the Beatitudes, or "blessings," the author of the
Gospel According to Matthew offers us a rich stew of elements—
compassion, humility, self-denial, charity—that Jesus believed
must be present if a life is to be lived in true obedience to the will
of God.

Jesus understood that in his time, as now, many people had
become unmoored from the faith of their fathers and mothers.
Some no longer practiced with any diligence, while for others who
did it had become rote, ritualized, desert dry, and lacking the depth
of joy or conviction. To Jesus' way of thinking, the situation called
for a return to the laws of ancient Judaism—the laws that had once

provided the bedrock on which a community of faith was first built. But the laws needed a new interpretation, one that went beyond strict legalism to capture the true spirit behind them. (This is why, as you may recall, in the body of the sermon we often read the refrain "You have heard it said . . ." followed by "But *I* say. . . .") What he was after, I think, was not so much the founding of a new religion as the revival of an old one, one he introduces most boldly here by reminding his audience that evidence of such a revival can be seen only when those who are the most cursed among us—the poor, the meek, the hungry, the persecuted—are the most blessed.

These blessings, these eight little verses, are an extravagance of wisdom in an economy of words, for nowhere in all of Scripture are we offered a more compelling image of a life of faith in a world of doubt than in the Beatitudes. Rooted in the texts and traditions of ancient Judaism, they crystallize the very heart of a message God has been trying to convey to us from the beginning of time: a blessed life is a life transformed, and blessed lives gathered in community are capable of transforming the entire world.

But if this is the case, why, with such a rich trove of great teaching that was available to him, the centuries of wisdom embedded in history and imparted from generation to generation through the ages, did Jesus speak *these* words and not others? How is it that above all others, he chose these passages to capture the spirit of his message, reflect honestly God's will for creation, address the needs of his generation, and remain pertinent to ours? These are the kinds of questions that determine the durability of any sacred teaching, and to answer them I think we have to start by considering three things: the life and times of the man himself, the people who loved him, and those who didn't.

A Ministry of Modest Origins

If it's true that we're judged by the company we keep, then Jesus was certainly among the most reviled men in ancient Galilee. After all, what else can we say about a man who counted in his coterie tax collectors (and other criminals), beggars, lepers, prostitutes, peasants, and the demon possessed? A man whose parents were unwed, whose disciples were unschooled, who entered the world in a borrowed feedbox, and exited in a borrowed tomb? When we scrape away the filigree and frill of later generations we're left with one unvarnished, inescapable truth: This was very much a ministry to society's common: the unadorned, the despised, the dismissed, the disrespected, and the dispensable.

They were Jews living under Roman occupation and situated for the most part in the region of Galilee (what would today be considered northern Israel, west of the Sea of Galilee). They were largely poor, largely earning their living off the land or the sea, and relied heavily on their learned rabbis to teach them how to apply their Scriptures to their everyday lives.

They were a people who harbored a collective history of exile and deportation, of being governed by nations other than their own, of paying enormous taxes to support a society from which they derived few benefits, and of laboring day and night on behalf of those who derived many benefits. Their life expectancy was shorter than that of the moneyed class, their infant mortality rate considerably higher. Their living conditions were noisier, more crowded, more dangerous, and less sanitary. Their children received an inferior education, entered the workforce at a younger age, and nurtured few dreams of social advancement. All of which can only leave us wondering where on earth they found the will to bear these burdens and live these lives, because although there are times when assurance from religion guarantees refuge from despair, the first century was not necessarily one of them. At least not for Palestine's spiritually downtrodden.

Dashed Hopes and Difficult Times

They had been promised much over the years, these people from whose ranks he came, but they had little to show for it. In the covenant promise made by God with their patriarchal ancestor Abraham, the nation that was to have been as populous as the stars in heaven was but a small and scattered lot blown thin across the arid landscape of the ancient Middle East, their majestic temple now defiled with sacrificial offerings in Caesar's name. They were governed by a king whose primary allegiance was to Rome and were counseled in matters of faith by a high priest who was paid rather handsomely to serve at the pleasure of a pagan emperor. On top of all this they themselves were at odds over what it meant to be a religious people; at one end of the spectrum, Zealots were calling for suicidal insurrections against the Romans, and at the other, Pharisees split hairs over minute legalisms. Meanwhile, off on the fringe were the ascetics, societal dropouts who retreated to live out their lives in the splendid isolation of desert caves. What's worse, the influence of Greek religious thinking was insinuated into the region at great peril to a traditional Judaism, whose strength derived from its theological purity. So much of the history of Judaism after Abraham received the covenant revolved around God's mandate that the Jews not mix with other religions (a common practice at the time) for fear of adopting some of those religions' beliefs or practices, and that was precisely the threat posed by the presence of the Greeks.

In the midst of such a swirl of competing assumptions, where *were* the people to find their refuge? How were they to make sense of their hardscrabble and unfair lives? Could they find meaning, hope, comfort, and dignity from a God who had spoken with such eloquence to their forebears but seemed silent to them? Who would awaken the echoes of glories past and wrest from the brink of irrelevancy a people who had been nurtured on Abraham's promise that God would make of them a great and mighty nation but who now lamented with the psalmist, "How long, O Lord; will you hide yourself forever?"

A World Turned Upside Down

It would be poetic here to say they believed Jesus to be the one to usher the clarion call, but it would also be presumptuous; a misreading if not of history then of human nature, because however eager we are to find our way to a better life, we're equally skeptical of anyone who guarantees us an inside track or a free pass. Then, as now, the landscape was littered with pseudo-saviors long on promise but short on deliverance; some no doubt well intentioned but not equal to the task, others oily charlatans hawking salvation on the cheap, still others probably certifiably insane. So on that desert day long ago when Jesus took to the mount to deliver what would become one of the most important sermons the world has ever known, preaching though he surely was to a polyglot audience that ranged from the abidingly hopeful to the deeply suspicious, they all had one trait in common: a cautious and extremely guarded curiosity about how, if at all, this man's message would be any different from all the rest.

He brought that curiosity to a swift halt with words that were sure to have unnerved some as they ennobled others: If you want to see what the kingdom of God could look like, if you want to live a blessed life, he told them, take the world as you know it and turn it on its head. That is to say, imagine it free of the tyranny, poverty, loneliness, and greed that now hold it in thrall. Imagine it loosed of the unholy trinity of ignorance, arrogance, and indifference that conspire to suffocate all remnants of hope. Imagine the hungry fed and the just vindicated, the poor satisfied and the pure sanctified. Imagine a world governed by an urge for compassion rather than a will to power. Imagine all this, he tells them, *because this is what God imagines*, because these are the people God has deemed blessed and this is what God wants us to make of ourselves. Imagine such a world, he told them, and then, having imagined it, live in accordance with it. Live it into being. Live as though the world *is* turned upside down, because when you do you will see the kingdom, if not come, then at least coming.

Had he stopped his sermon with the last beatitude his words would have been more beautiful than useful, a poetic embroidery of "what ifs" and "if onlys" that would do little more than tease the people with dreams of a better place deep within their hearts but well beyond their reach. But he didn't, and this is why his words are so potent. The Beatitudes are prologue and eternal essence; they are the vision that becomes validated, exemplified, made flesh and blood, if you will, by the instructions that follow them. The Sermon on the Mount moves from divine possibility to human enactment, first by painting a picture of what a blessed life is to look like and then giving us a sense of how to nurse it into being. True blessedness, Jesus tells us, includes things like reconciling yourself to your accuser, turning the other cheek, loving your enemy, being more righteous than the Pharisees and more humble than the silent saints, letting your light shine before others, and offering your prayers, alms, and fasts in humble solitude. To live a life contrary to the vicissitudes and vagaries of the world is to be with God. It is what Helen Keller described as fidelity to a worthy purpose; to paraphrase St. Paul, blessedness means being not conformed to the world, but rather transformed by the power and knowledge and love of God.

It was not a new language Jesus spoke to them that day, but an old one with a new dialect, for Jesus culled his words from the wisdom of the ancients—the prophets, psalmists, scribes, and rabbis—who had preceded him and were now immortalized in sacred Hebrew texts. He took their wisdom to heart, lifted it up before the people, and dared them to accept it in its most raw, most radical interpretation. Don't just live your lives in accordance with the letter of the law, he taught them, but with its very essence. Embrace the words themselves but beyond this, *divine the intention behind them*. Immerse yourself in that intention, let it penetrate your inmost being, wend its way into your soul, and then emerge from you in attitude and action. When you're asked to walk an extra mile you'll walk two, not because it is written but because you will be compelled to do so, because it is who you are as a child of God, because God walks with you, and because in so doing you will be living a blessed existence in a world turned upside down.

The Blessed Life Defined: Being, Giving, and Receiving

The heart of Jesus' message is the assurance that God had not been hiding from the people but was to be found in the sanctity of a life well lived, if not in the greatness of a nation then in the goodness of its people. He paints a picture of the kingdom not as a resting place where reclining angels preside over a perfect world, but as a restive place where, with God's blessing, common people do their best to redeem an imperfect world. It is not something we wait for but something we create.

As I hope to show in the chapters that follow, to the Jesus of the Beatitudes, faith compels action, which in turn deepens faith. Together they spiral ever upward toward illimitable heights of possibility. As Dag Hammarskjöld wrote, "the path to faith is through a world of action," to which we could add the reverse as well: the impetus for action is through a life of faith. Each beatitude not only embodies this idea but in so doing also anticipates the entirety of Jesus' adult life. His ministry, his death, and his resurrection, as the ultimate expression of the marriage of faith and works, are presaged in these verses, and I also hope at times to show the ways this marriage presents itself as well.

Attitude and action, faith and works. To paraphrase the great preacher Harry Emerson Fosdick, any time we wed faith and work we let our conscience get the better of our desires. We do so any time we act with mercy, kindness, sacrifice, or conscience to others, be they near to our heart or far from our daily preoccupations. We do so any time we comfort an old friend in her sadness or allow her to comfort us in ours. We do so any time we repair relationships long damaged by petty anger and malign neglect, or either offer or accept apologies for old hurts, or let compassion override pride in dealing with people we find difficult. In short, *any time we take the status quo and turn it upside down*, we are weaving together these two threads of the blessed life.

I think of what the prophet Zechariah said to the Hebrews when they asked him if they should fast to show their thanks to God for the restoration of the temple. Never mind your rituals, he told them, if you truly want to be closer to God, try "showing kindness and mercy to one another" (Zechariah 7:9). This is a durable piece of advice, one that comes to mind when I reflect with great admiration on the anonymous heroes among us who show their thanks to God in the quality and conscience of the work they do. They are volunteers who care for indigent AIDS babies in local hospitals, and community organizers who dedicate themselves to the herculean task of restoring dignity, decency, and hope to our inner cities. They are doctors who forsake the safety and comforts of a quiet practice here at home and work instead in poor areas of America or put themselves in harm's way to heal the wounded in civil wars fought on other continents. They are police and firefighters who race into collapsing buildings in search of lost causes or frightened people. And they are the social protestors—the pinprickers of our collective conscience—whose concern is human justice and who take it upon themselves to resist ill-conceived policies and immoral laws and then encourage us to do the same. Wherever we refuse to remain silent in the face of the pain of another human being, wherever angels make possible what devils make necessary, where soft we blow upon the embers of compassion to warm a steely cold and troubled world, the blessed life is coaxed into being because it is here that we are truly being agents of God on earth. The philosopher Søren Kierkegaard wrote that "to love another person is to help them love God," and I believe the Beatitudes attest to this as well.

But the reverse is true, too, and by this I mean we stand blessed with God when we give of ourselves to others but no less so when we *receive* another's kindness. One is the fundamental expression of our charity, the other of our humility, and both are equal measures of who we are. When we receive we acknowledge that we depend on one another more than we might otherwise care to admit, that we cannot live without one another's love, that we need one another to help us find human fulfillment. By daring to do this, by standing in humble openness to the mercy of the other, with gratitude as our only armor, we reflect the essential nature of our relationship with God, for what sustains us in our faith but God's mercy and our willingness to receive it? In this way receiving becomes a profoundly holy moment, a moment of incarnation, a moment when the person who gives is to us a small sip from the cup of a God whose love is forever poured out for us. This is why it is blessed to mourn, to hunger, to be poor, and I believe the Beatitudes attest to this as well.

Wherever Two or More Are Gathered . . .

There is one other element in all this, and it is what Martin Luther King Jr. called the beloved community. We need to remember that Jesus wasn't simply speaking to a small group of close friends when he delivered his Sermon on the Mount, but to the multitudes. He was teaching them what it means to be in right relationship with God and with one another and how these two are intertwined, but by implication he was also teaching them how to live and work together to change what God confides to us to change.

To believe in the Beatitudes is to believe in the strength of communal love (not the selfish sentimentality of a passing romance, but the irresistible force of a love so great that one person would lay down her life for another). It is to believe that that strength is sufficient to wear down even the most entrenched institutions of human hatred. And I believe *Jesus* believed that when love is galvanized against the powers of injustice, then a love harnessed rather than dispersed is a love respected rather than scorned. Like the soaring arches of the great temple that buttress and support one another, members of the beloved, blessed community do what no verse can do in and of itself; they rise and meet one another, hold one another aloft, strengthen and sustain one another, and in so doing create the heavenly canopy under which God's work on earth can surely commence.

But Do These Words Endure?

The Beatitudes' strong sentiments were certainly appropriate for an age long since past, but do they hold water for a civilization so very much more complex than that of the first century? In ancient days, before the conquest of Canaan and the founding of Israel, the Hebrew people were a loose confederation of tribes living in a small corner of a largely unexplored planet. In Jesus' time they were more settled but still largely isolated from other cultures.

In modern times, however, the many different cultures throughout the world are ineluctably bound together—whether we like it or not—by science, technology, and the pursuit of the intellect.

Many of the totems and superstitions of early beliefs have been largely dismissed. We are closer than the ancient world would ever have dreamt to understanding how life is created, and more efficient at devising ways in which it can be destroyed. To paraphrase Einstein, all's changed—except, that is, our way of thinking.

The world *is* infinitely more complex and promising today, but the truth is we have yet to shake the same problems that daunted those who lived in Christ's time. Suffering still makes poverty a tragedy, while wealth makes it a sin. Wars are still designed by the mighty and fought by the weak. People are still persecuted for what they believe, who they love, or what color their skin happens to be. There are times in our own lives, as in lives past and generations long ago, when we ourselves must strain to detect the faint whisper of God's promise above the din and demands, the broken shoelaces and broken promises, that fill our days.

Despite all this, or perhaps because of it, the words we call the Beatitudes are no less important today than when they were first uttered. They remind us that the world is not perfect and may never be; that there will always be those—ourselves included—who must mourn, or hunger, or thirst, who suffer poverty or persecution, for this is the nature of a fallen creation. But through it all, when we extend ourselves to one another, when we dare to love and be loved by another, when judgment is supplanted by mercy, pride by meekness, venality of intention by purity of heart, when we allow these moments—be they great or small—to arise and happen in our midst, whether we know it or not we have begun the sacred work of living the abundant, blessed life to which God has called us.

I hope that, in its own modest way, this book gives you even a hint of what that blessed life might look like for you.

Surrender

Blessed Are the Poor in Spirit

> *I like to go to Marshall Field's [department store] in*
> *Chicago just to see how many things there are in the world*
> *that I do not want.*
> —Mother Mary Madeleva, CSC

*I*t seems somehow fitting in a Gospel as rich with parable and paradox as Matthew's that Jesus' glorious sermon should open with this puzzling phrase—a variation on a blessing from the prophet Isaiah (55:1–2)—that rattles our logic by raising more questions than it answers. After all, it's one thing for Jesus to declare the poor in spirit to be heavenly blessed, but quite another for those hearing or reading these words to decipher precisely who they are. Were they the psychologically depressed? The religiously apostate? The morally destitute? The materially deprived?

The answer to these questions may have depended on who was hearing this sermon and how they heard it. Let me give just two examples. First, let's imagine that in the crowd that day we find one of Palestine's prosperous merchants, say, a trafficker in fine silks and linens. Let's imagine him a self-made, self-satisfied, self-assured man of means who earns his living off of beauty and then surrounds himself with it. He lives on an enormous estate whose entry is graced with carved marble and whose stables are filled with fine horses. He travels extensively throughout the Mediter-ranean, throws lavish holiday feasts for grateful friends, dines with kings, and counts hundreds of workers in his employ. Moreover, he fancies himself a man not only of taste and bearing but of rectitude; he abides the laws of the temple, attends worship regularly, and sees to it that a portion of his riches finds its way to the poor. So what is poverty of spirit to a man such as this?

Well, perhaps he hears Jesus' words and thinks of the times his own spirit has been laid low by personal misfortune; a business deal gone bad, his youngest child's mysterious illness, the death of a friend, or dark, disturbing doubts about how he's regarded by his peers.

Perhaps it's the occasional melancholy he's disposed to when he thinks of one day growing old and forgetful. His mind's keen edge has been dulling lately. He's been losing a step or two to younger men, and it has him worrying whether he'll be able to keep up with changing times. He can't be sure if the flattery his friends bestow on him is good-hearted or patronizing. Or maybe it's none of this, maybe it's the diminishing happiness he's finding in the riches he worked so hard to earn. Maybe celebrations have lost their excitement for him, and fine wines no longer please his palate. Whatever the case, his smile is a little forced now, his cheeks sallow, his sigh of satisfaction a little shallowed.

Perhaps poverty of spirit is impervious to wealth and therefore irrelevant to any discussion of the injustices of class distinction; it is not a thing of the purse but of the heart and mind. He hears the preacher's words and believes one day the sadness that seems to be insinuating itself into his soul will be somehow lifted, his step will be light again, and he will still be the man of eminence he's dedicated his life to becoming. I am the poor in spirit, he thinks, and my kingdom is in the offing.

He may well be right, but before we jump to his side of the aisle let's consider how the same words might've been heard by someone else who was there that day, someone of lower estate. Let's now imagine that somewhere else in the crowd is a seamstress, a woman in her late teens, of little means, who works long hours with primitive tools in the manufacture of beauty for the pleasure of others, her days spent hunched over this merchant's fine linens. It is a daily tease for her, this work that she does. She is so near to elegance, close enough to touch it, smell it. Indeed, she even creates it, only to have it slip through her weathered hands at day's end in exchange for a few meager denarii, about seven cents' pay at a time when an average worker earned ten times that amount. Her fingers are gnarled and her back bowed. Her eyesight is bad and she is old beyond her years. She returns home each night to a tiny one-room brick hovel where the roof leaks and there is never enough firewood. She has scant resources to feed her two children, let alone herself; and she worries about where the money will come from to pay this year's taxes.

The preacher tells *this* woman that the poor in spirit are blessed, that the kingdom will be theirs, and she glories at the prospect of a life lived beyond the hell of poverty and all she associates with it, for to her poverty of spirit is a lack of things, but it is also the degradation and diminution of self-worth that accompanies that lack. It is trying to be a good provider to her family but knowing that as often as not she will come up short and feel the chafe of personal failure in the clutch of her throat, or seeing the little pleasures enjoyed by other households and despairing over how she can explain to her children that she cannot afford so much as a piece of candy or a simple toy at holiday. She despises people's pity yet depends on it for her survival, so each time she accepts the benevolence of strangers she feels her fragile pride whittled ever thinner. She's angry at them for this, though of course she's really angry at herself. But now she hears that all this will one day be but a dim and dreary memory because a better time beckons, a time when her needs will be seen to, her family provided for, her dignity restored. I am the poor in spirit, she believes, and the kingdom is at long last mine.

Neither Jew Nor Gentile, Nor Free Nor Slave . . .

So who, then, are these forlorn, deprived, fortunate souls now ordained to find their rightful place in God's kingdom as the blessed poor? Is the poverty Jesus speaks of a matter of economics, or does it take on a more sublime meaning here, one that encompasses all variety of our unmet needs, visible and invisible? Does "the poor" refer to the merchant? His minion? Or is the poor someone else there that day, someone else whose heart churned with faith and doubt, or love and fear, or joy and sorrow? Is it you? Is it me? Can I, say, live my middle-class life, enjoy my modest comforts, sing my occasional bourgeois blues about bounced checks or late car payments and at the same time count myself among the blessed poor? If so, what does this say about my responsibility for those who truly lack even the most basic necessities of life?

I believe we find in Scripture that when all is said and done spiritual poverty has absolutely nothing to do with material poverty—and absolutely everything.

Poverty of spirit, as Jesus learned, as the psalmists wrote, and as the rabbis taught, is not a rejection of things per se but a repudiation of the power they have to control our lives, to dictate who we are. By this I mean if I am poor of spirit I turn my back on all culturally bound measures of my wealth and worth and pay no mind to human standards of success or failure. Spiritual poverty means I stand empty before God and naked to the world with absolutely nothing to either commend or condemn me; I refuse to see myself as the sum total of the heft of my resumé or the paucity of my credentials, the breadth of my riches or the extent of my debt, the quality of my friends or the disdain of my enemies. I could be a graduate of a distinguished university, of a local night school, or an eighth-grade dropout; the president of my country club or captain of my factory's bowling team; live in an exclusive neighborhood, a row house, or a prison cell—and it would not matter. I could hold down a prestigious job at a Fortune 500 company or scrub that company's floors at night, could eat in fine restaurants, hash houses, or soup kitchens.

In spiritual poverty I can declare with full faith and confidence that I will not be defined by the car I drive, the reputation I hold, the company I keep, or the dinner party I did or did not get invited to, because spiritual poverty is *liberation from the authority I assign to these and other things to serve as a measure of my worth, and the faith and willingness to look elsewhere for it.* This is why this first beatitude follows so close on the heels of the story of Jesus' rejection of the temptation by Satan, who took him to a mountaintop and offered him "all the kingdoms of the world and the glory of them." All that the world has to offer is never sufficient for us to purchase our goodness in the eyes of God, and so we are oddly freed from such fruitless strivings. Or, as Francis Bacon put it, "Money is a good servant, but a bad master."

But as Henri Nouwen once pointed out, we cannot be liberated *from* something without being liberated *to* something else, cannot simply die to one reality without being born into another. So if I refuse to define myself by what H. L. Mencken called the "surrounding and concealing superficialities," of wealth, status, pedigree, and the like, where does Jesus direct me to find my identity? In a competitive, consumptive, results-driven culture such as ours, how do I respond to the question of who I am, where my worth lies, without pointing to what I've done? The answer, of course, as easy to acknowledge as it is difficult to accept, is grace, divine kindness.

The Empty Professor

The Buddhist teacher Ram Dass, a former professor of psychology at Harvard, tells the story of a vision he once had while spending an evening at a friend's house. He was still on Harvard's faculty, and still went by his given name, Richard Alpert. He was looking into a mirror when, although dressed in suit and tie, he saw himself in his academic robe. "Ah, yes, Richard Alpert, professor," he mused, "haven't you accomplished much in your few years on earth," only to have the image melt before his eyes. "Well," he thought, "it's a nice identity, but I suppose I could live without it if I had to."

He looked again, and this time he saw himself on his sailboat in Boston Harbor. "Why there's Richard Alpert, bon vivant," he said to himself, only to have *that* image melt as well. "That's a good one too," he thought, "but I suppose if I really had to I could do without that as well."

Alpert looked a third time and this time saw himself surrounded by his family of birth. "There I am as the son of my parents," he thought, and when that image melted away he said, "Richard Alpert, son. Now that's a tough one to let go of. But I suppose I could."

Finally, he saw himself as he was, only to have that image melt away and leave nothing there. "Well, this is it, isn't it," he thought. "To give up Richard Alpert. To be totally empty. To have nothing. Can I do that?" As Ram Dass he has been asking himself that question ever since.

It is ultimately the *un*merited love of Almighty God that defines us and gives us enduring value, and here's how:

Grace is an inspired dance between the human and the divine. It is God's promise that we are eternally worthy not because of the contours of our identity but despite them, that we are loved human beings not because of *who* we are but *whose* we are. It is a love not measured or meted out but fully and freely bestowed, falling like a summer rain on parched earth, bathing and renewing the just and the unjust alike.

Grace is God loving Herod in his malevolence as he does Mary in her beneficence, Pilate in his cowardice as St. Andrew in his courage, the merchant in his splendor as the seamstress in her tattered rags. It is God loving you and me in *all* of these incarnations, from our highest aspirations to our basest motivations. In the words of Paul from Romans 8, "neither death, nor life, nor angels, nor principalities, nor things present, nor things to come, nor height, nor depth, nor anything else in all creation, will be able to separate us from the love of God," to which in this day and age he could have added, "nor IQs, nor IOUs, nor SUVs, nor second homes, nor third mortgages, nor social contacts, nor rap sheets, nor fancy clothes. . . ."

There is often a wall of differences that separate us from one another, but by accepting divine grace, by *accepting our own acceptability and the acceptability of others,* we find the window in that wall because we no longer see ourselves or one another as first and foremost a lawyer, ditchdigger, or vagrant, querulous neighbor or estranged friend, hero, villain, or victim, class clown or brooding loner, middle-born or favorite son, but as children of God who deserve to love and be loved for one simple reason: The Creator has called us to be a part of creation, has woven us into the sacred tapestry, has declared, "Let us make them in our image," and has deemed it good. We are the handiwork of the Divine; the unconditional love of the holy, Wholly Other. God has made us from the dust of the earth. Dirt poor.

It is grace, free and unmerited acceptance, that is, at root, what all of us are called to absorb in our hearts and reflect in our lives.

To Give, and Give, and Give Again,
as God Has Given Thee

Now that we've distinguished spiritual poverty from strictly material want, let's unite them again, for what is the substance of our love if in loving the needy we merely wish for their happiness but don't work for it? There are more days than I care to admit when in my own moral torpor I turn a deaf ear to the frenzied screeds of the indigent man in the park across from my home pontificating on every topic from Armageddon to the New York Mets. There are days when I turn a blind eye to the desperation of the thousands of innocents living in refuge from just the latest in a long line of uncivil civil wars throughout the world, and others when I decide to buy the shoes that are stitched together by a Central American sweatshop laborer—the modern-day equivalent of our first-century seamstress—who is probably a child, working sixty hours a week and paid about three cents for a product that will sell for five thousand times that amount. At such times as these I comfort myself with the myth that though I do care about these people there will always be someone else to lend a hand, write a check, or raise a voice in protest. God loves them, I don't have to.

But by doing this I am mistaking spiritual poverty for moral bankruptcy, reducing the former to a kind of gauzy idealism that shifts the burden of the poor from my shoulders to God's and relegates me to the role of a benign but ultimately indifferent spectator who doesn't want to define himself by his material comforts but doesn't want to part with them either. It's enough for me not to care about the possessions I have, I tell myself, there's no need to part with them for the sake of others. As the Trappist monk Thomas Merton noted, "Human nature has a way of making very specious arguments to suit its own cowardice and lack of generosity."

But the Bible—less apt to tell me what I want to hear than what I need to know—will not countenance my cowardice, so it's at moments like this I find the Hebrew prophet Amos's excoriation of the hypocritical faithful shooting back to my memory like a stab of light in a long darkened room: "they sell the righteous for silver, and the needy for a pair of sandals—they who trample the head of the poor into the dust of the earth, and push the afflicted out of the way" (Amos 2:6–7a).

Or if not Amos, then the apostle James, so deft was he at teasing the conscience of the religiously self-assured: "If a brother or a sister is naked and lacks daily food and one of you says to them, 'Go in peace, be warm and filled,' and yet you do not supply their bodily needs, what is the good of that?" (James 2:15–16).

In other words, my good intentions and well-wishes are scant substitute for the hard work of human love; they've never been known to fill an empty stomach, heat a cold home, or provide meaningful work for the unemployed. If I am to try and live in a state of blessed poverty, a disposition of detachment from the comforts of this world, then I must find a way to part with some of that comfort for the sake of those whose lives are so bereft of it.

It's right about here that I wish I could speak about the abiding sense of peace I get from living my life, as if I were a good Shaker, in material deprivation and voluntary simplicity; about the ease and grace with which I surrender all that I have for the sake of the poor, about the seamless integration of my actions with my beliefs, and about how well suited my family and I are to ascetic living. I would like to do that, but it's not the case. Nor, I suspect, is it for most of us.

We live in a culture that both molds and reflects our material values, one in which yesterday's wants become today's needs, where, as the writer Roger Rosenblatt observed about our consuming tendencies, "the thrill of the present drags you into the want of the past and then propels you into prayers for the future," where a person's value is a function of how much they have rather than what they *do* with what they have, and where the purchase of a fifty-thousand-dollar wristwatch, a $2 million boat, or an eight-hundred-dollar bottle of wine is more likely to breed admiration than disdain.

This attitude is both scandalous and unhealthy in its smugness; scandalous because there is no logic, however tortured, that can morally reconcile great wealth to grim poverty, and unhealthy because the desire for riches is an insidious, relentless thing that digs deep. It burrows slowly into our souls, feeds on and enlarges

The Price of Poverty

What would it take for the average American family to live the lifestyle of the poor of the world?

Begin by stripping the family home of its furniture. Beds, chairs, lamps, TV sets, silverware, *everything*. Leave them with a few blankets, a kitchen table, and a wooden chair. Take the clothing bureaus *and* the clothes. Each family member can keep one article of clothing, and only the head of the household is permitted a pair of shoes.

In the kitchen, take all the appliances. Leave a small bag of flour, some sugar, and salt, a few moldy potatoes, a handful of onions, and a dish of dried beans. Then, take away the meat, the canned goods, the crackers, the candy.

Next, strip the bathroom, shut off the running water, and turn off the electricity in the house.

Then, take away the house itself.

But this is just the start, it doesn't include the lack of telephone, newspapers, firefighters, hospitals, paved roads, or doctors. It also doesn't include the fact that the nearest school is three miles away, reachable only by foot, and consists of two classrooms.

Finally, money. We will allow our family a cash hoard of five dollars, which will prevent the family breadwinner from experiencing the tragedy of the Iranian peasant who went blind because he could not afford the $3.94 he mistakenly thought he needed to receive admission to a hospital where he could have been cured.

This is poverty. Blinding.

—Robert Heilbroner

itself, often when we're not paying attention. When we allow our enticements to grow and ripen they eventually crowd out our steadier thinking, skew our perspective, and arouse in us a niggling, unflattering envy. We begin to find that it's always the family on the next rung of the ladder, the one just beyond our grasp, the family just down the block in the slightly better neighborhood with the slightly bigger house that has the lifestyle we think we're entitled to. We aspire to their illusion of happiness rather than our own, but even if our ambition is realized our thirst is not quenched. Like Fitzgerald's Gatsby we ascend to a new plateau only to find that we've dragged our old compulsions with us, and from our higher vantage point we see with even greater breadth the riches that are not yet ours. But we lose sight of the fact that as we spiral higher we are distancing ourselves ever farther from the poor whose lives are lived so close to the earth, whose hopes take flight only in fantasy or fickle dream, who would so greatly benefit from the deserved generosity of our begrudging love.

I remember a patient I treated, whom I will call Linda, who once drove home this point to me in a rather poetic way. Linda was a brilliant, battle-tested young woman with a no-nonsense, close-cropped haircut, impeccably tailored clothes, and a fierce dedication to her work. She was one of those inspiring American success stories; she was born to poverty, went to school at night, landed an entry-level position in a large and prestigious investment firm, and gradually worked her way to a high six-figure salary, a second home, a generously feathered nest egg, and a low-level depression.

In one session, as Linda and I were knocking around ideas as to why she was so unhappy, she told me about a dream she had had the night before. "It was a chilling, raw winter's day," she started. "I was on the street in the neighborhood I grew up in, and my hands were cold. In short order I found a clothing store, went in, and bought a pair of gloves. Normal enough so far, but then something strange happened.

"I left the store, started down the street again, found another store, went in, bought *another* pair of gloves, and put them on over the ones I was wearing. I did this two or three times, until I could not only not feel the cold, I couldn't feel anything."

We stopped here.

In this terse psychodrama Linda's unconscious was trying to alert her to what she had lost as a result of what she had gained. As her professional success carried her farther away from poverty it also carried her farther away from the poor, from the people she had grown up with, the pleasures they had shared, the lessons they'd learned, and the problems they endured. Insulated with unnecessary layers of comfort, she forgot what it meant to be in need, to do without. She might still *know* of poverty, but she could no longer feel it or feel the pain of those who strain to meet their bills, feed their families, and deliver the goods on a child's birthday. Linda had become, literally, out of touch; her talent and grit had rescued her from something her heart and soul now wanted her to reexamine.

To her enormous relief and credit, she did. Of her own volition, Linda went back to the old neighborhood, rekindled some cooled friendships, involved herself in a community renewal project, and helped subsidize the education of a young girl who held the same promise and faced the same obstacles that she had years ago. She began to live a little more simply too, and it was a good exercise for her, because while she still enjoyed a very comfortable lifestyle she found wisdom in Jack London's observation about his own wealth and excess: "I could sleep in only one bed at a time, and of what worth was an income of a hundred porterhouse steaks when I could eat only one?" Linda was slowly transformed by willfully entering into a different relationship with her riches, loosing herself from the trappings of wealth, allowing herself to give more freely to others, and binding herself to the memories of her youth. As, layer by layer, the gloves came off, she came ever closer to touching the blessed kingdom of the poor in spirit. And she brought others along with her.

I found her experience not only telling of what we're capable of but also emblematic of what we're susceptible to, because for as long as I can remember it's been the case (as studies support) that in the United States the most generous among us are also the poorest, and as our incomes grow our generosity inexorably diminishes. At its worst extreme our gestures become little more than token sacrifices that reinforce an inflated belief in our own munificence. But God has a funny way of sneaking backdoor justice into our lives, so just when, like Linda's gloves, we've draped our consciences in enough layers of rationalization, along comes one of God's little agents to remind us of how much we yet have to do to approach the true freedom of biblical poverty. For Linda it was her subconscious. For me it was Oseola McCarty. Perhaps you know her story.

Born in 1908, a black child of the segregated South, Oseola McCarty spent eighty of her ninety-one hardscrabble years laboring for others, washing, drying, and ironing the clothes of the well-to-do of her hometown of Hattiesburg, Mississippi. When Oseola was eleven an aunt took ill, and Oseola left school to tend to her aunt's needs, which were considerable. Shortly thereafter she began taking in laundry to make ends meet. She didn't stop until her eighty-sixth year. A diminutive figure with eyes that penetrated you with their wisdom and soothed you with their kindness, Oseola was not given to complain much about the rigors of her work or the irony of spending so much of her time caring for clothes she herself could scarcely afford. Whether by design or necessity she lived simply in a tiny house her uncle had given her back in 1947, her quiet life revolving around her work, her friends (she never married), and her beloved church. She kept her Bible together with Scotch tape, she said, "so that Corinthians won't fall out."

When—after seventy-five years of taking in laundry for as little as two dollars a bundle—she retired, this woman who had given so much of herself to so many decided to give a little more. So in June of 1995 she wrote a check for $150,000 to create a scholarship fund at the University of Southern Mississippi—a school that would not have accepted her when she was of college age because of the color of her skin—in order that deserving young people who otherwise couldn't afford college would be given a chance to have the education she could never have. The Oseola McCarty Scholarship Fund represented her life's savings.

I suspect she was more than a little embarrassed by the attention that ensued; the newspapers ran their articles, the university sang her praises, and Hattiesburg locals stopped to shake her hand and remark in amazement at both her ability to save money and the ease with which she parted with it. In the first five years of its existence, eleven students benefited from her fund, and nearly eight hundred people and organizations made contributions to it. Quick to temper all the fuss, Oseola reflected with characteristic modesty, "I can't do everything, but I can do something to help somebody. And what I can do I will do. I wish I could do more."

Shortly thereafter, when she was invited to the White House, one newspaper could not have been more inadvertently succinct in capturing the essence of how little those of us with money in our pockets understand the motivations of the Oseola McCartys of the world, the poor in spirit who live and breathe the faith they proclaim with every bone of their bodies. When the paper trumpeted a trip she made to Washington, it did so with the headline "Dinner with the President Is Her Reward." I don't think it was. I think her reward came from somewhere else, and that in the quiet of her own home, when Oseola ran that Scotch tape up the spine of her precious Bible so that Corinthians wouldn't fall out, she did so somewhere in the vicinity of the ninth chapter and the fifteenth verse, where we read, "Thanks be to God for this unspeakable gift."

I don't know if I can be an Oseola McCarty. I don't know that I could ever be as strong as she was. But I do believe my family and I and those I love can carry a little bit of her into every decision we make that has repercussions, however slight or great, obvious or subtle, for the poor in our country and throughout the world.

I believe that virtue esteemed in principle can become morality achieved in practice. I also believe the reverse is true: that in endeavoring to do what we know in our bones to be right and just we draw ever closer to embodying God's will for our lives. The more we release ourselves from the false gods that vainly measure the fullness of life, the freer we are to count ourselves among the poor in spirit that Matthew speaks of in this beatitude.

To be poor in spirit is to know that we are all alive by the grace of God, that none of us has earned our way into creation, that we all stand firmly upon the same earth from whence we come. To be poor in spirit means knowing that we *do* need each other more than we may imagine, and that the joy of life is a gift to which all people are entitled equal access. It doesn't matter if we are a modest seamstress who finds inalienable love in her life despite the oppressive weight of poverty, or her wealthy boss who frees himself of that wealth to the end that that weight would be lifted from her back. When we are poor in spirit we receive God's love only to then surrender it again to others, heeding the words of critic and essayist Edmund Wilson, who defined love as "the only thing we get more of by giving it away."

And so we do, every time we reject the superficialities of difference that distinguish us from one another by embracing the inherent goodness and dignity of every human being. We do so every time we do with a little less so that others can have a little more, or resist the sanctification of a luxury by anointing it a necessity, or put food in the mouths of the hungry but also question why they have been made to live this way, or refuse to purchase goods made by the hands of exploited labor. Every time we tend to the need of the other before satisfying the desire of the self, we are inclining ourselves however infinitesimally toward the kingdom, and we are bringing others with us. It is these and other such wonderful, joyful, courageous, and foolish deeds that form the brick and mortar, the sweat and toil, with which the kingdom of the blessed poor will be built.

3

Empathy: Blessed Are Those Who Mourn

*Fare you well, fare you well, I love you more than
    words can tell.
Listen to the river sing sweet songs,
To rock my soul*
— Robert Hunter, "Brokedown Palace"

Jesus knew well the transitoriness of life, his own being caught up in a maze of uncertainty from the moment he was born and his parents took flight out of Bethlehem for fear of their child's safety, to the anticipation of his death at an early age. He had no visible means of income and did not know from night to night where he would lay his head to sleep. In response to their following him, he offered his disciples little in the way of security but much in the way of risk, and in response to their anxiety about the future he told them only to consider the lilies of the field. Scant comfort, that. He understood perhaps more than anyone alive that living entails loss, watching the things we cherish slip away, but at the same time provides an extraordinary stage for us to act out our love for one another.

Loss as Concrete and Metaphoric

Our lives are lived in a series of lives and deaths, comings and goings, gains and losses. In order to enter the uncertainty of the world we must exit the security of the womb, must, as the novelist Louise Erdrich put it, "no longer live beneath our mother's beating heart." It is with that first moment, that first glorious breath that we let loose our primal wail, our annunciation, the one with which we surrender any hold we had on our mother as the lone source of our existence. As our claim on her body gives way, so too does *her* claim on ours, to the state of pregnancy that she has lived for the past nine months. In this dramatic, painful, joyous, reluctant manner, life begins, with two beings engaged in the push and pull of beginning and ending, both compelled by nature to consummate it but both also, in some inchoate way, struggling with what they are losing for the sake of what they are gaining. It is in these first fitful moments that we begin to choreograph a dance that we will continue lifelong.

The baby meanders through infancy, grows into her childhood, and then one morning leaves home for her first day of school: an ending and a beginning. Over time she will make friends, lose them, and then make others. She will have her first fight, her first disappointment, her first betrayal, her first candy bar, her first crush. She may for a while believe in Santa Claus, and then she won't, but in its stead may grow to believe in the generosity of her parents. Experience will be gained, and innocence lost. She will for a time be convinced—as most adolescents are—of her own invincibility. Then one day someone young will die, and she won't believe in that any more either, but will be forced to reckon with the awesome power of human mortality. She will grow into adulthood and die to her youth; she will define her independence when she secures her first job, and her vulnerability when she loses it. She will learn to love, and perhaps lose that too. And she will love again. She may bear children, and if she does will be forever changed, a new being, a parent. Later still, gradually, imperceptibly at first, her body will begin to balk at doing things it once willingly agreed to, but with a little luck and a hint of grace her mind will learn to wrap itself around the dignity of old age, and she will live out her days remembering all that was gained, and all that was lost. What has transpired, and what yet awaits. As Katherine Anne Porter anticipated, "You even learn something on the day you die. You learn how to die."

Ever since Eden's gate swung shut we have played our part in a creation that spins itself earthward only to regenerate itself; one whose eternal rhythm is predicated upon, in the words of the author of Ecclesiastes, a time to build up, and a time to break down. Nothing lasts forever as it is. We are in a constant state of dying and emerging, for as the poet Stanley Kunitz put it, "unless the leaves perish, the tree is not renewed."

We're given ample opportunity to rue this permanent impermanence, times when we wish against reason and hope against hope that a good love affair or a long weekend or a steady-beating heart would never run its course, but the cold, unvarnished truth is they all do. Deaths, losses, the great ones and the little ones simply happen, and do so in their own time and at their own pace. They could be wise or wanton, abetted or imposed, prefaced by long hours of preparation or upon us like a hawk on an unwitting field mouse. They could be as welcomed as a long-awaited guest, or as resisted as an invading army in dark of night. The poplar grows twice as fast as the oak and lives half as long, and one man's marriage floats on love's wings for fifty graceful years while another's ends in a storm of recrimination in scarcely more than one. Loss is as predictable as it is uncertain, as logical as a mathematical theory and as arbitrary as lightning or the lottery visiting my neighbor's house but not mine.

Our salvation lies not in denying the inevitability of loss but in learning how to fold it into our lives, learning how to mourn, and, perhaps more importantly, how to *use* mourning.

Blessed Are Those Who Mourn . . .

When we suffer loss our lives are—if only for a moment or forever—disrupted, frozen in their tracks, and turned on their head. Loss blows through our bodies like a chilled breeze on a winter's day, catches us up short, pokes holes in our myths of invulnerability, demands that we look it straight in the eye and reckon with it. It forces us to alter whatever course, however well plotted, we've set for ourselves. Consider the following story, a moment in time that changed the course of one man's entire life.

In May of 1995 the actor and director Christopher Reeve was thrown from a balky horse in a bizarre riding accident that paralyzed him from the neck down. An accomplished sailor and pilot, an avid outdoorsman, a respected actor, and a vibrant father, at the age of forty-two he was confined to a wheelchair and a ventilator. Reeve faced the real possibility that he would never again enjoy the things that had given his life so much richness and meaning. It was, in his words, a totally arbitrary accident, a mere "instant of humiliation and embarrassment." He was truly a man of sorrow.

But in time perseverance bested pessimism and, with the support of people who love him, Reeve soldiered on and began the arduous task of rebuilding his life. With patience and good humor, he made the adjustments his body demanded of him, coming to terms with both the physical and psychological challenges his disability posed. He returned to work and has since been involved in a number of movie and theatrical projects. He became a tireless advocate on behalf of victims of accidents such as his, and created a foundation to advance research in the field of spinal cord injury and push for a cure. Having endured what might embitter others, Reeve believes his accident and its aftermath have provided him a deeper and more profound appreciation for his family than he ever could have imagined. As he observed in an interview a year later, his marriage was strengthened, his time with his children became richer, and he began noticing the little joys of life that he had long taken for granted. The task, he said, was to ask himself, "Not, what have I lost, but what life can I now build?"

As Reeve's story attests, mourning—the hard task of coming to terms with what we have lost—is an irreducible, irreplaceable piece of human life; it is a hub from which emanates the four spokes of recovery: emotion, thought, passion, and faith. Let me explain.

First, and at its most fundamental level, mourning is an emotional thing. It is the anger of loss, the denial of change, the dull thud of human grief that resides in the heart of a hungry child who has lost his mother's breast or an accomplished actor who has lost the use of his body. As they rail against the night at the injustice of their fate they do so to no end other than that they are expunging the poisons of their own private pain.

But mourning is more than this. It is also thought provoking. It is facing the ghosts of the past in light of the constraints of the present, allowing those constraints to serve as our daily reminder that nothing we cherish, nothing we hold fast, is ours forever. It is a sentiment that can either distract us from the beauty of the thing or compel us to cherish it that much more. For Chris Reeve his stilled body is both substance and symbol, his Damocles sword, his assurance, as if he needed one, that anything he cherishes must be embraced with the urgency of two lovers who hear the ticking of the clock above the beating of their hearts.

But it is more than this, too, because, as Elie Wiesel said regarding the suffering of the Jews during the Holocaust and the need to continue to speak out to prevent such horrors from ever occurring again, "the opposite of life is not death but indifference." Life is affirmed in grief because to grieve means something has stirred our passions, asked us to care deeply about it, given us the courage to give a portion of our heart to it. Love is painful because it risks loss; indifference is tragic because it risks nothing.

Finally, mourning is theological. God's covenant with Jacob didn't insulate Jacob from the loss of his youngest son to slavery, nor David his son to war, nor Mary her son to execution. Faith doesn't preclude loss but neither does loss preclude faith. Grass withers, flowers fade, but God alone stands on the right side of the eternal divide. The faint murmur we hear from that lofty place, the place the psalmist called "the rock that is higher than I," is that God loves us with a love that defies all finitude, even death, and what makes this so important is that for all the deaths we endure in life, God is never far from us. Indeed, mourning is nothing if not Good Friday from God's point of view—suffering defined as the prologue to redemption.

I do not believe it is God's benevolence when we escape suffering any more than it is his malevolence when we don't. God does not spook a horse, inflict one man with AIDS and spare another, is no more responsible for famines in Saharan Africa than for overflowing wheat silos in central Kansas, and did not lead some people into and others out of the World Trade Center on September 11, 2001. Life is arbitrary but God is not; God is not in the business of loading guns, breaking hearts, bankrupting families, dissolving once loving relationships, or destroying homes with a clap of thunder or a rush of rain. No, God does not engineer suffering and loss but rather calls us to redeem it, *to die into something.*

Just as the newborn baby lost the womb to be alive to the world, God bids us to find life emerging from deaths, what Tennyson called the little flower willing its way through a crannied wall to the light of day. When I think of what it means to die into something I think of my friend Mert Strommenn, an exemplary and loving parent whose son, in his early twenties, was killed by a bolt of lightning. "Irene and I wanted to make a meaningful gesture in David's memory," Mert told me, "so we established a fund for the training of youth ministers," a vocation his son had a particular talent for. "Don't get me wrong," he said. "It by no means made his death worthwhile. . . . But it made it worth *something.*"

What Mert is getting at is that in our sadness we can find threads of courage and strength, a flicker of hope that we can light the candle instead of cursing the darkness. And history does not teach us otherwise, for what lesser force could have compelled Picasso to give birth to *Guernica* in response to Spanish fascism, or Michelangelo to *Là Pietá* as a testimony to the suffering of our Lord? What but courage born of sadness emboldened Guatemalan activist and Nobel Peace Prize recipient Rigoberta Menchu to stare down death squads for the sake of indigenous Guatemalans, or a lone and anonymous student to stare down a fourteen-ton armored tank in the middle of Tiananmen Square? American racism was the birth pang for Maya Angelou's magnificent, haunting, and prophetic *I Know Why the Caged Bird Sings.* Chronic, incurable physical pain gave rise to the most eloquent of Emily Dickinson's poetry. And it was because of the death of Absalom that David wrote Psalm 23. Blessed mourners all.

In these and countless other deeply human moments the gold of hope is spun from the dross of mourning by people whose greatness is measured not by who they are but by what they've made

Empowering Sadness

Helen Hunt, author of *On the Nature of Consciousness*, once told me the story of how her young daughter turned fear and anger into mourning and compassion. Some years ago, the child had to endure the taunts of a schoolyard bully. "She had some rough encounters with this child," says Hunt. "We discussed it as a family, talking about how, by considering the pain in the bully's life, she could rethink her feelings toward him. The next day she went to school with a small religious medal in her pocket, a Christian 'icon' that she would reach for and rub between her fingers for reassurance that God was with her. When she got to school she steered clear of the boy and so did not allow herself to absorb his anger; but more than that, by keeping her distance she could contemplate the pain in his life and gradually turn her anger into mourning and compassion. In time, he even came, in his own way, to respect her."

out of their suffering. If these are not statements of faith, then I don't know what is, because what is the resurrection itself if not God's binding promise that we are all destined to emerge victorious over the ultimate loss, death *it*self? To make something out of our mourning is to create minor resurrections wherever we find life's cross hung.

. . . For They Shall Be Comforted

I do not think we can know how to comfort another unless we have first known how to mourn ourselves, cannot heal another without first understanding what it feels like to be wounded and broken. The offer of comfort from someone who has not tasted the bitterness of grief has a ring of inauthenticity about it. It's like a singer trying to sing a song in a language he neither speaks nor understands; his pitch could be perfect but the words would belong to someone else, as would the sentiment behind them. He's a mere parrot uttering sounds that mean absolutely nothing to him but are meant to move others. If I tell someone I know their pain, I must *know* their pain. It cannot be a rumor to me; it must be real to my experience and my language. To paraphrase St. Paul in his first letter to the Corinthians, I could give all that I have to another person, but if I don't have love, I really have nothing for them. Empathy is comfort's doorstep.

But empathy is risky business, which may be why we so often shy away from it. It's risky because when we extend ourselves to a person who is in pain we're allowing their condition to remind us of our own, remind us that what they are bearing is the *human* condition, and the inevitability to which we are all exposed. When recently I visited a cancer patient in our local hospital I could find space in my heart for her and her family because, having recently lost my mother after a long fight with emphysema, I know something about love and loss in my own life. We could talk and pray with gentle frankness about illness and all its attendant emotions, about the strain a family goes through at times like this, about the uncertainty, the frustration, the exhaustion, even the expenses and indignities they have to endure. That was the easy part. But when I left there, when I walked down the hospital corridors with their harsh fluorescent lights, fitful noises, and antiseptic smells, when I tread lightly by the darkened rooms and heard the muted cries of dying strangers intermingled with the whirs and beeps of the exotic machinery that was keeping them alive, I could not help but be struck in that instant by how evanescent the line of good fortune that separated me and my family from the fate that had come to visit this woman and hers. It is a line I could cross at any time and most certainly will quite often before my days are done.

Why then do we look after one another? Why, when it can be so wrenching an experience for us, do we bother to comfort another in her pain even as it reminds us of the inevitability of our own? Is it because we think of it as money in the bank, an IOU we extend in the hopes that others will be driven by guilt to pay us back in kind some day? Or is it superstition, a magical gesture that, like the wizard's curtain in the land of Oz, insulates us from the grim consequences of our own impotence? Perhaps it is either. Perhaps both.

Or perhaps not. I like to think that when it comes to another person's suffering we're compelled to do what we're inclined to ignore. I think of the people Jesus was comforting the day he preached the Beatitudes and how much loss they had suffered, collectively and individually. As a community they had lost their land, their governance, their ancestry, and their hope for preeminence in the world. They had lost their temple once, years before, and would soon lose it again. Most had lost their freedoms and some had lost their faith. They were no strangers to the jagged edge that has been known to rough cut its way through human history. As individuals most were scarcely better off; as Vincent Wimbush, professor of New Testament at Union Seminary (New York) notes, many had shabby homes, menial jobs, failed crops, and little hope. Security was a luxury enjoyed by others and envied by most, and women gave birth to ten children in order to have four survive, most of whom abandoned their childhood pleasures at an early age to work for their own living and find their own way.

This was a community whose sense of loss was precisely what Jesus was appealing to, for in this beatitude he draws his words from chapter 61 of the book of Isaiah, where the prophet paints an extravagant picture of a world of freedom and security born of the people's collective memory of their own oppression. Isaiah gathers the afflicted, the poor, the brokenhearted, the captive, the aggrieved about him and tells them that with God's help they will "build [cities] upon their ancient ruins and raise up their former devastations." They will wear "garlands instead of ashes" and be anointed in "the oil of gladness instead of mourning." It is the dust of the old that supplies the mortar for the new, the memories of pain out of which we wring the oils of gladness. We meet one another's sadness not with revulsion or relief but with kindness born of experience because there is no way other than this to foster the little resurrections, to build cities upon ruins, to make our deaths worth *something*. Said Paul Tillich shortly before he died, "I do not fear death, only dying alone; a death of no consequence." A death that means something is one that brings life to another, comforts another with the salve of its own wounds, as Jesus' wounded side did for Doubting Thomas. If mourning is Good Friday from God's point of view, comfort is Good Friday from Christ's.

But what does it mean to comfort and be comforted, to, as the poet Mariah Britton says, "fall, fall, fall, into the waiting arms of

God"? What's the flesh and blood of it in our everyday lives? Let me tell you the story of a man I know, Stan (not his real name), who had a small taste of this not long ago when he celebrated his fiftieth birthday.

Some of Stan's fondest memories are of his college days, and in particular of the four young men who were his closest friends. Together they shared their secrets, bared their souls, and confided their unbound ambitions in long late-night conversations, and upon graduation promised that although they were going off in different directions, they would continue to see one another as often as possible. Needless to say, it didn't happen.

"Oh, we stayed in touch for a while," Stan told me, "mainly to brag to one another about how much money we were making or how quickly we were shooting up the corporate ladder. But it all pretty much faded, and I missed them. So for my birthday I decided to round them up again, for old time's sake.

"What was so interesting, having not seen each other for so many years, was how differently we treated one another this time around. It didn't take us long to dispense with the business of how we'd each fared in our quests for success—we'd all done okay, I suppose—but then we began to probe a little deeper into what our lives had been like for the past twenty-five or so years.

"For the most part they'd been pretty normal—work, kids, mortgages, that sort of stuff—but the more I listened to these guys the more I came to appreciate what we'd all gone through, what everyone goes through just by living their lives; it's what I call the hard side of normal. One of us had had a bout with cancer, another had been divorced, and a third had just lost his job. My wife and I suffered two miscarriages before our first child was born, and both of my parents passed away when I was in my forties. There'd been a lot of water under the bridge for all of us, and it showed in how we interacted with one another. We asked more questions, and we bragged less. There were a lot of knowing nods when one of us would talk about tough times, and maybe even a tear or two.

"So much of our earlier lives had been predicated on taking the world by storm, making something of ourselves, maybe even outdoing one another," he went on, "but now, years later, I looked at the faces in that room and realized that I felt a kinship with these guys not just because of what we had each accomplished, but for what we had each survived; for the curves life had thrown us, throws everyone, and for our ability to love life despite its harsher lessons. We may or may not have taken the world by storm, but each in his own way had weathered his share of storms, and I really think that deepened and strengthened our love for one another." Small wonder, I thought, that the word "comfort" is derived from the Latin *fortiere,* "to fortify."

One of the things I love about Stan's story is the way the kindness the guys felt toward one another for all they'd been through didn't eclipse the festivities but simply backlit them; it showed me how pertinent this beatitude is not only in times of crisis or grief, but indeed *any* time I'm quick to dismiss another person's life as being too easily lived. To care for somebody *apart* from the immediacy of their experience, regardless of whether their days are spent brimming with hope, burdened with pain, or simply moving from one to the next with that remarkable uneventfulness that can alternately stifle the soul and soothe the senses, is to live a life of blessed comfort.

What Are the Steps to This Dance?

But what of those crisis moments? Just as the mother and her unborn child did their reluctant duet with its fits and starts, their farewell dance to the refuge of the womb, what is the dance *we* do when someone we care about is straddling two disparate worlds and not fully a citizen of either one? What is it, as the prophet Micah asked, that God requires of us?

A psychologist I worked with once gave me a piece of sage advice regarding a patient of mine. The patient was a bright young man, a chemist with a hefty education, brilliant insights, and no clue whatsoever as to the roots of his chronic unhappiness, adept as he was only at looking at his emotional life the way he might an intricate scientific formula, as a query to be solved. Each week he'd come to his sessions and speak with great, evasive eloquence about whys and wherefores, talk *around* what he was feeling about his situation, but never really hitting pay dirt, never tilling the soil deeply enough to get at the roots of his misery and what he could do about it. I talked with my colleague about this man, and will always remember what he said: "You know, that's the thing about intelligence. It can really get in the way of wisdom, the mind being such a good place to hide from all the messiness that comes with our feelings. Maybe what your patient needs to do is get out of his head and get into his heart. Stop thinking so much and let his feelings get the better of him, let loose with a good cry or a fit of anger, whatever it is that's stirring down there at that mysterious place he's so afraid to go to."

The more I thought about this, the clearer it became to me that he was talking about an emotional reluctance that had visited not only the patient but myself as well, because while he was content to puzzle around in circles, I was just as content to let him believe he could do so. From my standpoint our conspiracy was neat and orderly, risk-free, effortless, painless. But it was also pointless, and only when the two of us finally faced up to our behavior, only when the pain was uncorked and allowed to flow, fiercely unedited, was I able to be of some use to him and he to himself.

This episode reminded me that healing doesn't always entail problem solving or trying to find a way to minimize the other person's struggle. When my daughter skins her knee it serves no purpose to scold her for carelessness or assure her that her little wound is a minor blip in the greater scheme of things. Sometimes we just have to bleed with them rather than stanch the wound, sit with them, be undeniably, unequivocally, and irrevocably there for them in mutual helplessness. Hear each painful wail, each sodden cry as though it were our own. Sometimes misery doesn't just love company, it depends on it. Like the birthing mother and her emerging child it is a discrete but shared struggle toward one common end.

Do you remember what happened when Job endured his calamities and questioned why God would visit unspeakable pain upon such a "blameless and upright man" as himself? His friends— Bildad, Eliphaz, and Zophar, the Chaldean equivalent of the three wise men—came and "raised their voices and wept . . . and sat with him on the ground for seven days and seven nights." No words were spoken, the only sounds emanating from the four men being the muted groans of private agony, drifting skyward like sacrificial smoke from an ancient altar, inarticulate supplications to a distant god.

Job's friends were indeed wise to do what they did, to sit in silence, because they offered no answers, and because at least for those seven days Job knew he was not alone in the world and that his suffering was as inexplicable and unjustified to others as it was to him.

But then they opened their mouths, and when they did they closed off all avenues of love toward their friend. One by one they weighed in, like a council of inquisition, insisting Job's plight could only be rectified by owning up to whatever unnamed sins God was surely punishing him for. Needless to say, Job took little solace in their reprimands, and rightly so. What he wanted, what he needed, was neither explanation nor accusation. He needed their hearts; they gave him their minds. It would not suffice.

Turning our hearts toward those in pain is all they really ask of us. They don't want platitudes about how suffering is meant to wizen us or humble us or strengthen our character. They don't want to know that it is God's mysterious will behind the loss of the family farm or the family pet, or that the scales of justice will somehow, at some time in the illimitable future, tip in our favor with riches equal to what we have lost. Like the thief on the cross who, moments before death found him, found paradise in the person of the man who was hung alongside him, healing is most deeply felt when vulnerability is met in kind. As a friend of mine said some months after her husband died, "In the depths of my grief when people came to visit, I appreciated the ones with the good casseroles far more than the ones with the bad theologies." Or, as Bill Coffin observed, we are better for having mourned in the presence of those who comfort us than not to have mourned at all, because the entire experience reinforces our interdependence, the gift that we are for one another. Shared mourning is a thing without which we could not live.

For Whom Do We Mourn?

Our Scriptures offer us two accounts of Jesus being brought to tears: once over Lazarus and once over Jerusalem, once over a trusted friend and once a community of strangers, one befallen by a sickness of body and the other by an infirmity of soul.

In the first story, on the way to Bethlehem Jesus met Lazarus's sister Martha, who told him she feared that her brother was dead. Seeing the pain etched in her face, as John records in the shortest verse in all the Bible, "Jesus wept." In her terror she asked that he draw upon his power to save her brother from death. Instead he drew upon his weakness to bring him to life. He cried with her, bound himself to her with the not so small bond of shared grief and abject sorrow, and for a moment in time they were united by a force far greater than any that might try to come between them. I believe it was from this comforting, fortifying grief that Jesus found within himself the strength to restore his friend, because the real power this man held was not the power of a magician who could heal with sleight of hand as no one else could, but the power of a profoundly human being, whose healing power came from his ability to care about people, as any one of us could. If this story teaches us anything it is that the seeds of healing (derived from the Old Saxon *helian,* meaning wholeness, or life) lie in the deep, rich soil of compassion. When we are so humble as to get down on our knees, run our fingers through that soil, tend and feed it, water it with our tears, feel it cool and moist between our fingers, we too realize that we all tread upon this same earth, live with the same fears, hopes, losses, and loves, and in this commonality have the power to keep one another whole.

But as imperative as it is that we love one another in this way, it is also not enough. The real challenge lies in our ability to extend that love to such loveless places as the modern-day equivalents of the Jerusalem that Jesus wept over, places where people we don't know are enslaved to others, where, as he said, despots "bind heavy burdens and lay them on others' shoulders, but they themselves will not move them with their finger" (Matthew 23:4). Whether it is by making a phone call on behalf of a political prisoner or offering a prayer for her freedom, writing a check to a cause that is near to your heart or a letter of condolence to a person who isn't, every time we give of ourselves in this way we are upholding this beatitude by caring for people to whom we are bound by nothing more than a shared sense of what it means to mourn.

"Blessed are you who mourn, for you shall be comforted." Breathed there ever a soul more acquainted with the two edges of this one blade than the man of Nazareth, the one who upon his own cross of grief could still comfort his mother? This is what this beatitude is, isn't it? It is the cross, the crossroads, where necessity meets opportunity, the place where redemption is defined by the intrinsically human need to suffer loss and the uniquely human capacity to turn that suffering into love.

4

Patience: Blessed Are the Meek

I am not interested in picking up the crumbs of compassion from the table of someone who considers himself my master. I want the full menu of rights.

—Desmond Tutu

Meek, as in Weak

I have never regarded meekness as a thing to admire or a quality to attain. The war in Viet Nam and the glorification of the warrior athlete in my youth, corporate takeovers, and the dissolution of public welfare in my adulthood have taught me that our culture consecrates the strong by castigating the weak. How odd it is, then, to consider the meek as world-beaters, inheritors of the earth.

Try as I might, I cannot conjure up so much as a single image that validates this blessing. The pharaohs have always ruled their domains with conscripted soldiers, the Caesars with centurions, and the Custers with cavalry. In the extreme, Hitler had his Luftwaffe, Mao his Red Army, and bin Laden his Al-Qaeda. On the commercial battlefield of the twenty-first century, business executives fancy themselves today's warrior heroes. They've been bestowed with unbridled power and unseemly salaries to oversee kingdoms in which millions of peasants labor for as little as a dollar a day. Even our kids seem to intuit that crowns are bestowed upon those who prove to be the smartest, strongest, wittiest, prettiest, or most popular among their peers. So if indeed God has apportioned a parcel of earth for the meek to inherit, then it is in a corner of the world that I, for one, have yet to visit.

The Songs of the Psalter

But if I fail to see the rewards of this blessing perhaps it's because I don't fully understand the character of its beneficiaries. Exactly who did Jesus have in mind when he spoke of the meek? Was he referring to the timid, the feeble, the spineless, the "go-along-to-get-along" yes-man? Did he mean the reluctant businesswoman who lives in mortal fear of a contrary opinion? Was he thinking of the guy whose sole ambition in life is to taper his sails to the headwinds of the status quo and is content to live, in Tutu's words, off the crumbs of others? Or was his point—as some have suggested—that the godly Christian is the one who suffers in glad silence the degradations of this life so as to inherit a better one in the next? To put it bluntly, is meekness simply cowardice disguised as forbearance? The answer may lie in the old adage that every good teacher is an even better student: Jesus knew his Scriptures.

When he included this beatitude in his sermon, Jesus wasn't inventing a new idea but recalling an old one, one he'd first heard as a young boy. It was part of what we now call Psalm 37, a poetic treatise on faith-based patience written six hundred years earlier for an Israelite community in exile after losing their land to the mighty Babylonians.

The psalmist's audience, like Jesus', was a band of outcasts who quaked at the thought of being swallowed up by their enemies, so to their fears he counseled patience leavened by resoluteness. He urged that they be calm but steadfast before those who "draw the sword and bend their bows, to bring down the poor and the needy," not because it was their fate in life to suffer unjustly, but because in due time their enemies' "swords shall enter their own hearts, their bows shall be broken," and "the meek will inherit the land." Through the psalmist, God was speaking with the force of a feather and the weight of a hint to a lost community whose obedience would be rewarded when, years later, they returned victorious to the home of their birth.

Moreover, the author of this psalm is but one in a long line of biblical writers who commended their followers to trust in the power of patience and the wisdom of calm. The prophet Amos praised the same morality when he told the meek they were more honorable in God's eyes than the corrupt politicians who "trample the head of the poor into the dust of the earth" (2:7), and Isaiah correctly foresaw the defeat of an invincible enemy army when he told of its overthrow at the hand of a God who "will put an end to the pride of the arrogant and lay low the haughtiness of the ruthless" (13:11). Later, in the epistles, James equates the meek with those who are "doers of [God's] word and not only hearers," and Paul counterposes a life in vain pursuit of wealth and fame with one "aimed at righteousness, godliness, faith, love, steadfastness and meekness."

Simply stated, *biblical meekness is quiet perseverance in the face of brute rage; it is our staunch refusal either to lay down in submission or to rise up in violence before those forces that oppress us.*

In other words, meekness is a lot to ask of us. In order to better understand what meekness means in our own lives, we need to

The Sage of South Africa

Godly things come in small packages. In the darkest days of South African apartheid, Anglican bishop Desmond Tutu used to lead groups of followers up to a scrubby promontory high above Capetown called Table Mountain. It was an otherwise unremarkable place, except that from here they could look out on the Atlantic Ocean and see Robben Island, the penal colony that held Nelson Mandela and a great many other leaders of the resistance movement. With armed police scrutinizing his every word and the island hanging like the crucifix above a makeshift altar, Tutu would remind his people that the relentless drive of Christian love would one day prevail over the repellent might of human hatred, and this nation that they had worked so hard to build would indeed be free. It was at one and the same moment an act of worship, of renewal, and of defiance; a gesture of faith, ultimately vindicated by the power of persistence.

reflect on the three key elements inherent in my definition: oppression, perseverance, and nonviolence.

Who Is My Enemy?

Sadly, our world has no shortage of people conspiring to do one another ill. Eastern Europe is still in the throes of a decade of strife born of national rancor, cultural hegemony, and political instability. The Middle East is ensnared in a bewildering array of competing interests, rooted in entrenched fears and justified by tortured religious logic. America's once noble war on poverty has become an ignoble war on the poor. Children as young as ten years of age are not only carrying handguns into their classrooms, but using them. We never seem more chastened at the danger of creating enemies, only more proficient about how to attack them, and so we needn't look much farther than the front page or the eleven o'clock news to find instances in which one group is trying to oppress another.

But oppression can be as subtle as it is obvious. It can insinuate itself into affairs private as well as public, so that even those who seem to lead the most charmed lives can be beset by caprice and cruelty known only to themselves. I remember one Sunday some years ago when I preached a sermon about the church's need to respond to the housing crisis in New York City, where the waiting list for public housing alone has nearly a quarter of a million names on it. It was an issue our church had been historically ambivalent about, and the church leadership was hoping to kick start some interest.

After the service, one of our church's more affluent members, a straightedged, middle-aged, blunt-speaking businessman I will call Walter, buttonholed me and said, "Reverend, it's awfully difficult for me to care about anyone else's troubles right now, so I hope you won't be disappointed if I don't give too much thought to this little issue of yours. Y'know, you can still be in hell with a roof over your head."

Now, knowing Walter to be a man of some means, a steady job, good health, and a seemingly happy marriage, I had to ask what it was that was troubling him, and he told me. "Here it is," he said in his inimitably laconic manner, "I've got a boss breathing down my neck, a teenager who won't talk to me, a stock portfolio that only goes down, and a cholesterol level that only goes up. Next week, my mother-in-law has an appointment with an oncologist, my brother with a divorce lawyer, and my wife with a judge in traffic court! I'm sorry folks are waiting for apartments in this town, I really am. But right now my heart's so loaded down with my own pain that I have no room for anyone else's." Clearly, for Walter the burdens of the world were no farther away than his own doorstep and as real as the burdens of those who have no doorstep at all.

Walter's litany of woes was useful to me because it reminded me that the brute rage that results from human oppression can be found anywhere, from the broad stage of world affairs to the narrow plank of one man's "hell with a rooftop," and in places as evident as an inner-city housing office or as deeply hidden as the furrowed brow of a well-dressed man. Beyond the sting of poverty or the strain of war, beyond the calamities that upheave whole populations, beyond border skirmishes, back rents, and gang bangs, oppression is writ small in the dozens of daily indignities that try our patience and erode our calm: in the scratched fender, stubbed toe, cancelled meeting, missed train, lost bet, check that didn't come, bill that did, and two-year-old with the sore throat.

The Conscience of Resistance: Dorothy Day

Dorothy Day, the indefatigable founder of the Catholic Worker movement, wed patience to persistence in her lifelong quest for an end to the arms race. One of the ways Dorothy exhibited her resistance to warfare was by refusing to pay any income tax, citing the fact that over half of it went to pay down the debt of past wars or the prospect of future ones. One night at a public debate, her opponent cited Scripture in an effort to unmask a fallacy in her reasoning. "Didn't Jesus say to his follower," the opponent began, "that we must render unto God what is God's, and unto Caesar what is Caesar's?" to which Dorothy replied, "My friend, if we rendered unto God everything that is truly God's, there'd be nothing left for Caesar."

Who is my enemy? From an audience of millions to the deepest reaches of my own heart, my enemy is any oppressive force that, by inches or by yards, threatens to diminish me as a human being. Which is precisely why we must persevere in the face of the enemy's might.

Water on Granite

"If you can't be optimistic," observed Bill Coffin in 1979, "then at least be persistent." Persistence is the marriage of discipline to patience, and Coffin, then senior minister at Riverside Church, knew whereof he spoke. Having just returned from visiting fifty-two U.S. hostages being held in revolutionary Iran, his words were instructive to an anxious America because he understood that in times of crisis there is a human inclination toward defeatism, and defeatism is the preamble of despair. When our adversary seems so hard to confront and we so helpless, we shrink from the possibility that time and effort could whittle the odds until they are in our favor.

But indeed they can. Let's not forget that there was a period in our own nation's history when women were the property of their husbands and blacks the property of whites, when Jews were barred from public schools and blue-collar workers were forbidden to organize into unions. A time when exercising your right of free speech could cost you your life's work, and the homeless were deemed criminals by virtue of their poverty alone. These were not just attitudes, they were laws. They are all gone now, whittled away by the prayers and petitions and marches and sit-ins of thousands of ordinary people who, if they did not optimistically believe that by fighting for what is right it would come to pass, were at least persistent in the belief that if they didn't it wouldn't. In persistence the saints have made possible what the sinners have made necessary.

Now a story of the saintly possibility of human persistence: Some years ago I had the opportunity to spend time with a family whose only child, a three-year-old girl named Annie, suffered from autism. Autism is a particularly cruel affliction because it renders a person virtually incapable of building relationships, accepting affection, communicating feelings, or even cuddling up in her mother's arms for an afternoon nap. In the face of such emotional isolation, I was truly amazed at how much love and attention Annie's parents showered on her even when they received so little in return.

"It's not as tough as it looks," her mother told me, "because we can't do anything less. We can't *not* do it, if you know what I mean. We give Annie our love because we hope that some of it, some little, tiny piece, seeps through. I don't know if it does or not, or even if it ever will. But I'll tell you this, whether or not we succeed, we won't stop trying." In giving Annie that love, they are inheriting their piece of the earth. While this story is unique unto the family, I suspect we can all reflect on times in our lives when we've faced both the hardship and the reward of reaching out and caring for someone who—because of anger or hurt or fear or some other reason known but to God—found it exceedingly difficult to respond.

The perseverance of Annie's parents, not unlike the perseverance of those who walked with Jesus to Jerusalem, marched with King to Birmingham, heeded Coffin's admonitions on Iran, or ever stood firm for a worthy cause, reminds me of the words of Italian thinker Giovanni Papini, who described the meek this way: "They are like water which is not hard to the touch, which seems to give way before other substances, but slowly rises, silently attacks, and calmly consumes, with the patience of the years, the hardest of granites."

The Moral Might of Nonviolence

Violence is like any other parasite; it starts out small and insignificant, has to replicate itself in order to survive, and poisons all that is healthy around it in the process. In Gandhi's words, "you start by taking an eye for an eye, and pretty soon the whole world is blind." This is why when we hear in the news of a fight breaking out, be it between nations, rival schools, or next-door neighbors, it's often reported as something that began as a minor incident—a scrape, or a bump, or a misunderstanding—that escalated into physical, poisonous, sometimes deadly violence. Indeed, who among us has not at one time or another felt the sting of another person's venom and wished them ill in return, only to come to realize that it's *our* anger, not theirs, that snakes deep into our blood, courses through our veins, weakens us, wears us down, and keeps this pernicious thing alive? The lingering anger I feel when a stranger insults me, a friend abandons me, or another driver cuts me off on the highway is not only pointless but dangerous, for as Augustine put it, "I am not so much afraid of being destroyed by my enemy as by my *enmity*."

But Augustine here also hints at violence's one critical weakness: it can't spread unless its target accepts the poison. If I am the host I must be predisposed to cooperate with my invader. I can get caught up in a cycle of violence only if I respond to it in kind. The civil rights marches of the late '50s and early '60s, like the freedom movement in South Africa years later, were successful precisely because the marchers refused to rise to the taunts of their enemies, refused to answer hatred with hatred when bottles were hurled at their heads and insults were hurled at their children, refused to plot revenge when turned on by police dogs, fire hoses, and surly mobs. Had they done so they not only would have surrendered the moral high ground that served so well to call attention to the depravity of their oppressors, but they would also have escalated their struggle into an all-out war that they were destined to lose. By refusing to provide the poison a place to take root and grow, by engaging in disciplined nonviolence in the face of unmitigated cruelty, they undermined the strategy of their antagonists, whose swords, in the words of the psalmist, "entered their own hearts," and whose bows, in due time, were broken. All of us have encountered instances of cruelty in our lives, and I believe when we look back on them we see it was those times when we refused to meet cruelty with hatred, when we somehow mustered the will to remain calm and centered and confident, that we overcame our pain rather than our pain overcoming us.

What is nonviolence? It is an article of faith. It is the willingness to endure the pain of oppression, steadfast in the belief that, as with any poison denied a place to take root, it will eventually, inevitably, dissipate, diffuse, and destroy itself. As Martin Luther King Jr. told the Nobel audience upon receiving the prize for peace in 1964, it is "the answer to the crucial political and moral questions of our time; the need for [us] to overcome oppression and violence without resorting to oppression and violence." The principle of meekness, ratified by the power of revolution.

Perhaps we can now say what meekness means in our lives. It is that which will not allow us to tolerate oppression, ordain submission, ratify injustice, or concede indifference. It abides by the power of the hand not raised in anger, and persists even in the absence of optimism. It refuses all impulses of retaliation, hatred, submission, victimization, or enmity. In meekness the water of patience grinds down the granite hatred of our enemy. It is Jesus of Nazareth crucified high upon a cross by those who saw him as a threat, and it is Christ resurrected, ultimately victorious, even over death itself.

Let us now turn our attention to the source of that water of patience, to discern how it is we can find within ourselves the power to be meek.

Meekness and Faith

It's admirable to think of the meek as possessing, in Giovanni Papini's words, "the patience of the years," but where exactly do we find that patience when, in the blink of an eye, a tempest can rise to stir our fears or stroke our anger? How do we stand alone before the brute strength of our oppressors? How have others?

The short answer, of course, is that regardless of the texture of our anguish we never stand alone, because to live in faith is to be entwined in an eternal spiral in which obedience on our part is fortified by assurance on God's. As the renowned preacher Harry Emerson Fosdick wrote, it's easy to find God in heavenly places, but important to find him in hellish ones as well: in a child's beaming eye but also in a beggar's vacant stare, in peals of laughter and in wails of sorrow, in the bosom of our family and in the twilight of our loneliness. Whether oppression is visited upon my own soul or my neighbor's, whether by the whim of nature or the cruelty of another human being, whether in great tragedy or simply accrued aggravations, choosing to stand and face it is an act of faith in which we become emboldened by the knowledge that when we do so God stands with us, "prepares a table before us in the presence of [our] enemies," not to weaken our struggles but to invest us with the strength to overcome them. This is so, I believe, because to strike the pose of justice is to evoke the will of God, and with meekness as our moral compass we tighten that spiral, binding ourselves more closely to God.

I also believe that if faith is summoned by our love of God, it is deepened by our allegiance to one another. The reason Jesus preached meekness to the multitudes is because he understood how in times of crisis a community can often summon the courage to do what an individual cannot. Alison Boden, a minister of gentle wit and exceeding generosity who holds forth from the pulpit of Rockefeller Chapel at the University of Chicago, once told me about attending an impromptu worship service shortly after her ordination. It had been convened for a group of inner-city tenants preparing to do battle with an unscrupulous landlord who wanted to evict them from their homes. Meant to fortify their souls for the struggle ahead, the service closed with an exhilarating rendition of Martin Luther's "A Mighty Fortress Is Our God." It was during this hymn, Alison said, that she couldn't help but believe that as they sang the verse:

> And though this world with devils filled,
> should threaten to undo us,
> we shall not fear, for God hath willed
> His truth to triumph through us,

they really did feel fearless, not only because God was with them but because they were with one another. "Because," she said, "God triumphs *through* us." Like individual voices, some timid and some bold, some woefully off-key and others dead-on, a great, insistent chorus rises together as one and demands to be heard.

For They Shall Inherit the Earth

Someone once wondered if, when the meek *do* inherit the earth, they will remember to remain meek. It's an interesting question that misses the point completely.

What are the meek destined to be? Pharaoh with a conscience? Custer without the cavalry? Benevolent dictators who, in Tutu's words, "simply offer to make the handcuffs a little more comfortable"? Or is there a more sublime dimension to Jesus' blessing, one that doesn't carry such imperious connotations?

Consider this story of the eminent psychologist Victor Frankl: In the dead of night, Frankl received a phone call from a distraught woman, who told him this was her final call before killing herself; having given up on her fellow human beings, he was her last hope. Frankl, being a good clinician, kept the woman on the phone, tried to offer her reassuring words, tried probing for the root of her despair, and finally got her to agree to come and see him the next day. He hung up the phone not knowing if she would indeed make it through the night, let alone show up at his office. To his delight she did, and when he asked her what it was he said on the phone that kept her from killing herself, she answered, "Nothing you said really made much of a difference to me; it was the mere fact that at one o'clock in the morning you would spend two hours with me, a complete stranger, that assured me all is not lost."

What Frankl did required neither genius nor valor, only humanity. He was simply a voice at the other end of a telephone, as any of us could be, speaking, like God above, divinely understated and immeasurably patient, to a lost soul longing to return home. It was something you and I are thoroughly capable of doing. When at long last his patience penetrated this woman's armor of despair, her hellish place became a heavenly one.

This is what it means to inherit the earth. It is not necessarily supplanting the rule of nations but planting the seeds of hope, and then abiding with them, protecting them from whatever storms may loom large on their horizons, feeding and watering and beseeching them, nurturing them into fruition. Inheriting the earth means wresting a piece of creation that has been ceded to the demons and reclaiming it for God.

A meekness that inherits the earth is tens of thousands of men, women, and children in Birmingham, Alabama, staring down their enemies for the irresistible principle of racial equality. But it is also a young couple loving a child who cannot love them back, a newly ordained minister taking up a cause that is not her own, or one stranger helping another find her way through the darkened gloom of an endless night. Meekness is a Massachusetts millowner named Aaron Feuerstein, whose factory burned to the ground just before Christmas in 1995 and who broke every tenet ever taught in business school by pledging to his thirty-four hundred workers that not one of them would miss a paycheck while the company was shut down. It is a man named Jack, a former patient of mine, who, long bothered by the self-centered life he lived, now makes a point of finding the loneliest, most unpopular people in his work-place and inviting them into his home for dinner. It is even poor Walter of the low portfolio and high cholesterol, miserable about his world falling down around him, but still coming to church, say-ing his prayers, and asking divine guidance. Common people doing uncommon things—this is the way in which the ordinariness of life, its drudgeries, hassles, indignities, and injustices, becomes transformed into something indeed holy. And worthy of living.

Meekness is any one of us, at any time and place, encountering a rage born of injuries as great as the subjugation of one people to another or as modest as a bad day in an otherwise good life, and persevering with steady calm and solid faith until such time as those injuries are consumed. As a Sufi sage once put it, "Like the divine mother who bears in her heart all of the pain of human cre-ation, we must bear that portion of the world's pain that has been entrusted to our care."

5

Self-Denial: Blessed Are Those Who Hunger and Thirst after Righteousness

We are to receive righteousness as a gift and pursue it as a task.
—Dennis Hamm, S.J.

There is an old story about a businessman who's in a terrible hurry to get to a meeting in another town. He flies in to the town's airport, rushes out the terminal door, hops into a cab, and shouts at the driver, "Drive like mad, I'm in a huge hurry!" The cabbie speeds off as ordered, but after a few minutes his harried passenger notices they're headed in the wrong direction, leans forward and asks in a near panic, "Where in the world do you think you're going?!" The cabbie answers, "Beats me. You just told me to drive like mad, you didn't tell me where."

So before we wrestle with the question of how to *get to* righteousness, let's begin by taking a look at what we mean by it. Where exactly *are* we going? Where are we asking hunger and thirst to take us? What was Jesus doing when he invoked a passage from Psalm 107, a song of gratitude for God's looking out for us in times of trouble ("For he satisfied the thirsty and the hungry he fills with good things") and altered it in this way, in effect telling his followers that in God's kingdom not only are the hungry filled but also those who, by all appearances, hunger for something more than the bread of the earth?

Righteousness, Not *Self*-Righteousness

Righteousness. It's not a word we hear very often in common conversation. It doesn't come rolling off the tongue at ball games or in barrooms. It doesn't receive a lot of play in, say, the idle chatter of two friends walking their dogs or waiting for the morning train. It's not heard a lot at the office water cooler. No, righteousness is what, when I was a child, I would have called one of those "Sunday words," by which I meant words we heard spoken with great gravity and reverence in church or in church school, but pretty much nowhere else. Like wearing my only suit or eating an elaborate dinner off the good china, there were certain things a kid was likely to encounter on Sunday that he wouldn't much come across the other six days of the week, and hearing the word "righteousness" was one of them. I think my perception hasn't evolved very far since then, and I often suspect I'm not in the minority on this.

If I had to guess, I'd say we still don't give the word "righteousness" much of a workout because its mere utterance conjures up strong images of a kind of monklike holiness that seems so different from and indifferent to the more rough-hewn way most of us live our lives. When I think of the righteous my mind's eye sees clear-eyed, beatific people who walk around deep in thought about profound things like love and beauty and truth, their sandaled feet barely scraping solid ground, their placid aura unshaken by the blare of a truck horn or the sight of a gum wrapper on the sidewalk. There is an otherworldly quality to these people, a serenity, a sense that they're floating down a stream that we're all fighting our way up. I don't think they worry about the same stuff I do, about whether the dry cleaning will be done by Friday, or the raise will come through, or the home team will win the big game this weekend. They're better than that. They're *righteous*. Holy. If their purpose in life is to inspire me to greatness, I'm afraid they succeed only in underscoring my own insufficiencies. At day's end, I could not be more different from them.

Nor could I be more wrong, because righteousness is not first and foremost about rectitude. It's about relationship, about being right with God, about trusting more in God's time, God's way, God's inscrutable wisdom than in our own.

In ancient times, with the warring Assyrians breathing down his country's neck, invasion imminent, and things looking terribly bleak, the prophet Isaiah could pray with the patience of the ages:

"O LORD, be gracious to us; we wait for you. Be our arm every morning, our salvation in the time of trouble" (33:2). Isaiah could pray this because he was in a state of righteousness, because, all evidence to the contrary, he would not abandon hope that God would redeem his chosen people.

So too Mary Magdalene. Filled with sorrow at the death of her rabbi, her leader, her friend, she nevertheless made the faithful journey to his tomb when no one else would, to anoint his lifeless body. In doing so she became the first Christian, the first person on earth, to learn that he had conquered death and was no longer there.

Or Paul. Because he believed God would ultimately triumph over evil, it was from the very belly of that evil, a Roman prison, while facing the real prospect of a horrible death, that he could write with confidence to the church at Ephesus: "that Christ may dwell in your hearts through faith, as you are being rooted and grounded in love. I pray that you may have power to comprehend, with all the saints, what is the breadth and length and height and depth, and to know the love of Christ that surpasses knowledge, so that you may be filled with all the fullness of God" (Ephesians 3:17–19). The brightness of heaven, glimpsed from the darkness of hell.

When logic dictates desperation, the righteous hope; when alienation, they seek; when cynicism, they love; and when oppression, they find refuge. As the psalmist wrote, "For you, O Lord, are my hope, my trust, O LORD, from my youth. Upon you have I leaned from my birth; it was you who took me from my mother's womb. My praise is continually of you" (Psalm 71:5–6).

What is derived from righteousness? *A state of existence wherein we give ourselves over to the invitation to covenant that God has extended to us.* It is by no means a perfect union, flowing forever with the tide.

However unique the contours of our lives, however different yours is from mine or mine from my neighbor's, I believe the one thing we do have in common is *some* understanding that faith is, by definition, our attempt to respond to God's having called us into being. I do not believe that at some arbitrary moment God simply blew life into our lungs and set us loose the way a small child sets a top spinning aimlessly across a wooden floor, for what would this reveal but a disinterested God whose creative purpose is no better served than that of an artist who labors mightily over a painting, only to walk away, indifferent, when the last stroke is brushed?

God is not disinterested. Rather, the unspoken message of life is that in calling us into being God has initiated a dialogue, a relationship of promise and responsibility that may well have begun long before the glint in our parents' eyes and may well continue long after our days on earth. God's initiative is the very germ of our being, the irreducible beginning of our faith journey, the seminal moment of what Dietrich Bonhoeffer called the "irresistible Yes." This invitation to covenant, to life, is *God's* righteousness, that is, God's *being right with us,* and the heavy labor of a life of faith is a matter of our learning how to reciprocate in kind, how to reflect back our desire—our hunger and thirst, if you will—to be right with God. It is by no means easy, and we are by no means perfect, but it is the task to which we commit ourselves lifelong.

Divine Subtlety: The God of the Exodus

The call to covenant relationship—God's gift and our pursuit, as Father Dennis Hamm, a Jesuit theologian, called it—was an idea not unfamiliar to Jesus and his followers; indeed, it was embroidered on their hearts and embodied in their history. For just as they themselves were subject to another nation's governance, so it was that generations prior their ancestors, an unremarkable little band of Hebrew slaves, sought their freedom from an empire they could not best in a land they did not know, led by a God they could not see but to whom they were asked to entrust their very lives. Their exodus odyssey is at the very heart of the Torah, the holiest books of the Hebrew Bible. Their forty-year wandering from the bondage of Pharaoh through the desert of uncertainty to the land of bounty, *their* seminal moment, is both story and metaphor, at once both an indelible moment in human history and a timeless portrait of the constant push and pull between divine promise and human hesitation, the steady pulse of God's righteousness and the quavering reluctance of our own faith.

Consider the story in this way, as recounted in the first five chapters of the Book of Exodus: It is the ancient Near East, and the Hebrews are an insignificant speck on the global landscape, an enslaved confederacy of loose-knit tribes useful only for their sweat and sinew as they endure forced labor, day in and day out, in the construction of a city that it is to stand as testimony to the Egyptian pharaoh's bloated self-importance. A God who wants nothing more than to see his people free must first convince a reluctant Moses that he is the one to lead them to the promised land.

Moses' resistance is formidable; he even goes so far as to suggest his brother, Aaron, as a suitable surrogate. "Aaron's a better speaker than I am," he tells his God. "More forceful, more persuasive. He's a lawyer, you know."

But God will have none of it, so, slowly worn down like a bedded stone in the desert wind, Moses eventually relents, with serious misgivings that are only magnified when, after he intervenes before Pharaoh on behalf of his people, the Hebrews are punished for their impudence by having to manufacture more bricks with less straw. The believers have their beliefs shaken and the doubters their doubts confirmed. Why should they entrust their lives to *this* god? And, it turns out, this is only the first in a series of strains on their ability to trust that God would indeed deliver them, for when the exodus finally does get under way it is met by one calamity after another.

A last-ditch assault by the Egyptian army at the Red Sea almost kills the liberation aborning, as does near starvation at Elim and then scorching thirst at Rephidim. Finally, at Sinai, there is the living dread that for all their struggles, the bush no longer burned. The fire was extinguished. After years of their wilderness wandering, God had left them here, abandoned.

Throughout the exodus story God's righteousness is represented by saving acts launched in the face of searing doubts; the attacking army is swallowed up by the sea, manna falls from heaven, water flows from rocks, and, when Moses finally descends from the mountaintop, he does so bearing ten laws that would serve as the foundation for a state that is still observing them to this day. In God's economy, at God's pace, in God's time, and in God's sometimes incomprehensibly circuitous manner, God's righteousness prevails. We do ourselves and our God a great disservice when we insist upon an earth-rattling clap of cosmic thunder to affirm our faithful inclinations. We are instead far better served when we wait with patience, work with diligence, and trust with confidence that, despite the calamities and plagues that might at any time occur, in the words of Arthur Ainger's immortal hymn of 1894, "God is working His purpose out, as year succeeds to year."

But let us not be too quick here to judge the ancient Hebrews' misgivings as evidence of a lack of faith, an inability to be "right with God." Indeed, who among us would be so quick to pay credence—let alone homage—to a god who foreordains struggle as a fundament to religious experience? No, if anything, the important point is that for all they endured, through so many years of illness, fear, doubt, and privation, they still managed to put one foot in front of the other. That they did this day and night lends credence to the belief that faith is not a clean and rising arc that sweeps neatly from the soul to the sky, but a sometimes messy, imperfect, and ongoing process of steps forward and back. Eyes one moment are fixed on the horizon and the next glancing askance over the shoulder at a road not traveled, a fitful trek. Only eventually, and with the accumulated scars of life lived, are we delivered to a better place.

For God to be right with us requires only that the invitation be extended. For us to be right with God, however, requires that we confront all the inhibitions and preoccupations that make less arduous paths more tempting than the strait and narrow down which we are summoned, through those times when God's bounty is close to us but also through those when it seems so far away. It's a matter of putting one foot in front of the other, no matter how hostile the surroundings, how tempting the alternatives, how diabolical the pharaohs, how sore those feet, or how far from home we seem to be.

I take solace in remembering that, as I mentioned earlier, just before Jesus came to preach the Beatitudes, the devil took him to

a mountaintop, showed him a world of untold riches and unparal-
leled power, and invited him to claim it as his own. Jesus did not
do so; he chose instead to walk dusty byways that would bring him
face-to-face with the poor, the mistreated, the malnourished, and
the misbegotten, to a wedding at Cana, the banks of the Jordan, a
woman at a well, a blind man at Jericho, the court of Pilate, the
upper room, the garden at Gethsemene, and finally to Calvary
itself, his portal to paradise.

No, righteousness is not first and foremost a matter of living in
a state of blessed detachment from the world's wonders and
hassles and challenges. It is a matter of discerning what it means
to be right with God in the very midst of them. Righteousness is
the odd amalgam of faith and doubt that allows us to put one weary
foot in front of the other even when we are anxious and frightened
about where these steps will take us.

So if it is this uncharted path down which we walk, how do we
use hunger and thirst as our companion for the journey?

Of God and Gods

The story goes that the Buddha was down at the river's edge when
a young man approached him and asked him what he needed to do
to attain enlightenment. Without saying a word, Buddha took the
man by the hand, thrust his head under the water, and held it there
until just before he was ready to pass out. He then lifted the man
out of the water, and said to him, "In those last few moments, what
were you thinking about?" "I was thinking about air," the man
said, gasping for breath. "Anything else?" the Buddha asked.
"No," the man answered, "I was just thinking about air; my life
depended on it." "Precisely. When you can turn your attention only
to the eternal truth, as if your life depended on it," Buddha told
him, "you will be on the path to enlightenment."

What is it that we desire? Where do we cast our eyes? An unfair
question, really, because in truth, for most of us the answer is a
moving target. When we are sick it is health; when poor, money;
when lonely, companionship; when troubled, peace. Like a bud

straining to the sun or a cub to its mother's milk, it is in our nature to desire and then to fulfill. We do this both to survive life and to enjoy it. But that's not really what Buddha was getting at, was it? What he wanted to know was what the young man desired *above all else,* what he hungered and thirsted for so intently that anything else was

> "There are so many hungry children in the world for whom the face of God appears as a loaf of bread."
>
> —Gandhi

a pale pretender to the throne of his unmet wishes. To paraphrase Richard Niebuhr, know the answer to this question, and you'll know what your god looks like.

While desire in and of itself doesn't carry a moral valence, the objects it points to and the importance we ascribe to them often do. Let me give an example, if in extremis, of desire gone mad. Back in the late 1980s the stock market was on a bull rampage and young gunners fresh out of business school were riding it for huge six-figure salaries. One of them, a man by the name of Dennis Levine, was riding high in one of the country's most prestigious financial firms when he was caught trading on "insider information," that is, information about a company that would cause its stock to rise or fall rapidly and without prior warning. Levine was busted for it, and the price he paid was a steep one. He lost his broker's license, his reputation, and two years of his life to a federal penitentiary. When he was released he was asked by a reporter why he took such a risk, and this thirty-five-year-old man who, just one year before his arrest, had earned over three hundred thousand dollars, answered, "I'll tell you why. I did it because I wanted to get at the *real* money." The real money. Money was not Levine's desire, it was his *god,* his idol. His air. It was that for which he felt the groan of hunger and the parch of thirst. Thus it is written, "Again the devil took him to a very high mountain, and showed him all the kingdoms of the earth and the glory of them, and said to him, 'All these I will give you if you will fall down and worship me.'" Money had become the object of Levine's devotion and worship, the thing for which he'd risk everything, the singular urge that stirred the question, "What do I have to do to attain you?" Having given his answer, he pursued it as if his very life depended on it. In many ways, it did.

At the other extreme, however, consider the story of Maria Skobtsova, a mid-twentieth-century Orthodox nun of Ukrainian birth who turned her back on the aristocracy (*real* money, in Levine's vernacular) into which she was born and made her way to France to work for the resistance during World War II. A short, cherubic, unprepossessing little woman, it was there in France that she and her life's cause found each other, dedicating herself to the poor and the homeless. It was there that she was imprisoned for the crime of rescuing Jews and smuggling them to safety, and where she committed her last charitable act on earth when, shortly before liberation, she willingly took the place of a Jewish prisoner who was being led to the gas chamber and there died a martyr for Christ. Asphyxiated, surrendering the very air that she breathed. Because *someone else's* life depended on it. Like Dennis Levine, Maria too pursued her cause, but if for him it meant filling his pockets, for her it meant emptying her soul.

I'd like to believe the world is as rich with saints as it is riddled with sinners, but I suspect that's not the case. I also suspect that neither saints nor sinners are emblematic of a life to which most of us either attain or descend. My guess is most of us walk the tightrope between the two, and it is somewhere in that precarious balance that we are looking for our righteousness, our right relationship with God. So how do we cast our eyes heavenward and still put one foot in front of the other without tripping over the clutters that are so much a part of our everyday lives?

Blessed Hunger

I don't believe the hunger and thirst Jesus speaks of in this beatitude pertain only to those among us who are literally without decent meals or daily bread, because I don't believe inflicted poverty engenders implicit righteousness. To be born in a state of material deprivation does not in and of itself bestow righteousness. Instead, I believe Jesus is telling us that hunger and thirst—that is, *a minimal portion of something we need to stay alive*—is a *means by which we can attain righteousness*, and what Jesus' message allows us to do is define our hunger as a conscious act rather than a misfortune of circumstance.

We satisfy desire much the way we quench thirst—temporarily. There is no well that, once having visited and drawn from, and, finding the nectar sweet and cool upon our throats, we are not eager to return to. If I have an experience I enjoy, I want only to enjoy it again, if not now, then at a later time. A good book comes to an end and I feel a slight twinge of sadness, parting with it as I would an old friend. I miss the companionship and pleasures it provided. I remember the good feelings the book engendered in my reading of it. I must find something every bit as appealing to take its place, and will not feel my hunger satisfied until this happens.

If it's not a book it is something else I've come to depend on: a favorite meal, the company of friends, a corner office, the respect of colleagues, a month's vacation, tickets to the show, the end of the week, or maybe just someone else to cook dinner. For a desire has only two criteria: it is something that gives me pleasure and something I am presently without. Or, as the French poet Alphonse de Lamartine put it, "Limited in his nature, infinite in his desires, man is a fallen god who remembers the heavens."

So what does it take to forget the heavens, if even for a moment, and to what end? Where do my needs end and my wants begin, and what do my yearnings have to do with righteousness? I must eat and drink, sleep and rise, play and work, earn and spend, must, in short, do all the things to which I've been naturally ordained and culturally accustomed. But God has made me capable not only of satisfying wants but of *experiencing* want, that is, experiencing— either by circumstance or volition—what it means to lack, to do without; and in so doing prove to myself that even if I have nothing more than my daily bread (as millions do) I can nonetheless survive.

It's not always easy to ride the carousel of our dreams with our hands tight upon the reins of our painted horse while all who are around us are grabbing for the brass, but I believe this is something of what Jesus is getting at in this beatitude. He tells us that hunger—that is, unmet desire, or more to the point, *choosing* to render a desire unmet—is a good way of being right with God. In hunger, he intimates, we deepen our appreciation for what we have by heightening our awareness of what it means to do without what we've long taken for granted (just ask anyone with a broken leg or a flat tire).

Be hungry, Jesus is saying. Live more simply than you have to, if only just a bit, if only every now and then, if only today. Put yourself in right relationship with God by putting yourself in right relationship with others. And put yourself in right relationship with others by putting yourself second and them first. Allow yourself a little less so that others might have a little more. Travel lighter than you might. Buy one less Christmas gift and give a little money to the poor. Watch one less television show and give a little time to your children. Pray for others before you pray for yourself. Cut out a meal this week, or maybe just a snack, and use your savings to pick up a few groceries for the local food pantry. Volunteer some time there. Visit the neighbor whom no one else can stand. Walk to work tomorrow for the sake of the air you breathe, let alone some exercise. Do what a friend of mine does once a week, and take a cold bath if only to remind yourself that you're *not* among the world's billions who, by necessity, do so every night.

Engaging in behaviors such as these is difficult at first because we're navigating a territory that is not only unfamiliar to us but antithetical to our common impulses. It's like finding our way around a strange room in the dead of night; it takes a while for our eyes to adjust and become accustomed to new surroundings. But over time, repeated often enough, we *do* become accustomed. We learn where to walk and where not to. We find our path, our straight and narrow, one foot in front of the other. At first perhaps we have more doubt than trust, but, over time, more trust than doubt. In due time we come to fully trust this new behavior, and we commit it to our consciousness; then it becomes as familiar and comfortable as an old pair of slippers. When this happens, when we internalize gestures of self-sacrifice so that they come forth from us the way ink comes forth from the poet's pen, I believe that is when we have begun to make ourselves right with God in two important ways.

First, in shifting the center of our gravity from ourselves to others, we give flesh and blood to the words of Tennessee Williams, who on his deathbed said "redemption happens when a person puts himself aside to feel deeply for another." Second—and this is particularly important for us Americans—we disabuse ourselves of the conceit that we are entitled by birthright to the disproportionate bounty we enjoy; that because it is good to have, it is better to have much; that the kingdoms the devil lays before us not only *can* be ours but *should* be. That it is okay to fell the timber or draw the oil or burn the chemicals or waste the cropland if it is all somehow to the betterment of our standard of living. Unmet desire humbles us by instilling in us a perspective that is more true to what it means to live in community with others than our baser wishes would have us believe.

In the long run it is this humility that may do more to "right us with God" than all our gestures of sacrifice and self-denial combined, because the hardest thing to shake is not the impulse to sate our appetite for nice things, but the ego that remains well fed less by the doing of good deeds than by the praise we get from others for having done them. As Jesus reminds his followers a little later in this sermon, "Beware of practicing your piety in front of others in order to be seen by them. . . . [W]henever you give alms, do not sound a trumpet before you, as the hypocrites do in the synagogues and in the streets, so that they may be praised by others" (Matthew 6:1–2).

A Unique Kind of Hunger

Finally, let's take this verse at face value and consider what it means literally to hunger for the sake of righteousness. Let us consider the act of fasting as a way of drawing closer to the divine.

Biblical tradition has it that whole communities engaged in public fasts, often to purify their bodies, quiet their lives, and repent of their sins. Both Moses and Elijah fasted in preparation for their private communions with God, Ahab did so to feel more humble before God, and immediately after his baptism Jesus fasted to prepare for the extraordinary ministry to which this same God had called him.

We are so often busy with the necessary preoccupations of life—phone calls to return, meetings to attend, groceries to buy—that as often as not we reach day's end feeling as though we've fed ourselves a steady diet of fast food that's rendered us overstuffed and undernourished. But when injected into this syncopated mayhem, fasting can be a time of conservation and replenishment, of removing ourselves from the din around us long enough to discover that while we are needed in the world we are not indispensable to it.

There is something transfixing about fasting, in part because when we do fast we find there is so little else we *can* do. Stillness enfolds us. Quiet envelops us. Simplicity surrounds us. Problems that might at other times breed rancorous days and sleepless nights are gently released the way tension in a rope is released when a gnarl of knots is slowly undone. We are, as the Chinese poet Lui Chi put it, "alone with the beating of our heart," and it is into this stripped-down world, this room now emptied of all the distractions that otherwise fill our day, that the moment comes when God appears in quiet peace to keep company with us.

It is not, of course, that God "enters us"—the way a stranger enters a place where she is long expected—so much as that we are now disposed to discover that God has been there all along. Whether we fill that moment with prayer or study, song or meditation; whether we contemplate the earth's sorrows or celebrate her wonders, give thanks or ask forgiveness, remember the past or forget the present, sit alone or with others; this time is the sacred occasion in which our emptiness allows us, as Pierre Teilhard de Chardin observed, to leave the surface and, without leaving the world, plunge into God.

It is a good thing to fast from time to time because it reminds us of the very fundament of righteousness, that God justifies us neither by virtue of the deeds we've done nor by the brilliance with which we've done them—that is, our actions speaking to God of our goodness and worthiness—but by the disposition of faith that is eloquently symbolized by our emptying of ourselves and allowing God to speak to us.

The Zen of Emptiness

"Blessed are those who hunger and thirst after righteousness, for they shall be filled." This is a wonderful paradox, really: to be emptied of our strivings for what Dr. Raymond Gibson called "lower-case gods" to the end that we might be filled with faith in tenuous times. To surrender our preoccupations and live in God's economy, to wander the wilderness, one foot in front of the other, and believe that manna will fall, rocks will spring water, and a promised land will be built by people as expendable as an ancient slave, as common as a Galilean carpenter, as filled with the fruit of human possibility as you or I.

Contrition: Blessed Are the Merciful

*You have not lived a perfect day unless you've done some-
thing for someone who will never be able to repay you.*
—Ruth Smeltzer

"Build yourself a spartan society," warned the Reverend Greg
Sutterlin over a couple of beers one night, "and you'll breed yourself a generation of gladiators." He was talking about a community suffering from a deprivation of goodness, not goods; one
where wealth abounds but the whims of the rich best the rights of
the poor; where one group is elevated above another because of the
size of their house or the family of their birth; and where conformity is esteemed above freedom, retaliation above forgiveness, the
love of power above the power of love. When human kindness is
subverted to the grandeur of the culture, he argued, what we're left
with is a population of obediently loveless people.

The Roman Empire of Jesus' day grew materially strong but
spiritually weak, and when it collapsed it did so under a succession
of warring emperors. The British Empire crumbled because it
lacked the moral authority to force its version of civilization on
peoples who valued the integrity of independence above the
authority of a distant throne with an alien culture. The same hubris
doomed the Dutch. At the extreme edge of imperial arrogance we
find the regimes of Stalin, Hitler, Somoza, Pinochet, and
Milošević, all of whom confused fear with respect, to ruinous end.
Indeed, when we walk the sinuous road through all those years of
human history, from the ancients to the medievals to the moderns,

we see everywhere the wreckage of one society after another, one empire after another, one pretender after another. Each could have been so much more than it was had it not confused indomitable love with incurable weakness. As God admonished the Israelites in Deuteronomy: "You were unmindful of the rock that bore you, you forgot the God who gave you birth" (Deuteronomy 32:18).

As for Jesus, in the Scriptures he studied he came upon the word "mercy" over 150 times, as either descriptive of God or instructive of us. In his world vengeance came more quickly than forgiveness, and punishment more frequently than pardon. An eye for an eye was the rough equivalent of retributive justice. The imperialist thought nothing of taking the life of a slave for the mere sport of it. Mercy was a lesson easily lost, and I believe this is one reason Jesus singled out the merciful for blessing.

Nor should the lesson be lost on us.

We're Number One?

We Americans are not so far removed from the Rome of Jesus' day in one respect: we are a nation of superlatives. As they did before us, we laud the biggest, fastest, boldest, and best; the tallest, coolest, smartest, and first. We root for the winners and forget the rest, cheer for the champions and hold ticker-tape parades for hometown heroes. In sport we fete the winner of the big game and in business the closer of the big deal. We don't so much encourage our kids to indulge in the elegance of learning for learning's sake as we urge them to get the highest grades in their class and elbow their way into a prestigious university. As a nation we reserve our lowest rung for those whose income is dictated by charity and our highest for those whose wealth is granted by inheritance (its own form of charity). On the world stage we fancy ourselves the strongest of all the nations, although we are far from being the most civilized: our per-capita prison population is greater than that of most industrialized countries, as is our incidence of handgun violence, and we lag behind industrialized countries in per-capita expenditures for things like education, health care, and prenatal care. We legitimize this myth by means of the costliest and dead-liest arsenal of military hardware in the history of the human race; we are the world's gladiators.

All of this makes for a skewed sense of works righteousness among us, of a sense that our worth is directly defined by the sum total of our accomplishments. We've so institutionalized competi-tion that it's become a bedrock of who we are. We put enormous pressure on ourselves to be triumphant at the expense of being car-ing, and in the process we make mercy a poor stepsister to meri-tocracy. We make it too costly to commit errors, admit mistakes, fall short, not know the answer, ask for a second chance, ask for directions, or ask for forgiveness, let alone hope that forgiveness will be granted. Perhaps this is why something as fundamental as mercy has to be codified in a biblical text: it is such a delicate thread in a culture's mesh, a fragile thing so easily dismissed by societies in too great a hurry and ignored by people under so much pressure to do well that they've forgotten how to do good.

This myth that we should be measured only by the greatness of our works is further fostered by the fact that with the pursuit of per-fection comes the illusion of freedom, of soaring like Icarus to heights both seductive and dangerous. We come to believe that the better we are at something—the more talented a professional, more clever a wag, more imposing an athlete, or more intelligent a muse—the more we will find doors opened to us and the greater a share of life's bounty will be dropped at our feet. But I believe the reverse is true, and this is the nub of this beatitude.

The more willing we are to embrace our *im*perfections, our flaws, and our shortcom-ings, the more liberating our

> "Teach me to feel another's woe, to hide the fault I see; that mercy I to others show, that mercy show to me."
> —Alexander Pope,
> *The Universal Prayer*

lives can be because we free ourselves from the tyranny that ensues when each victory means only that in the next race we'll have to run faster. It is in self-acceptance that the seeds of mercy are sown, where, like one plant sprouting two shoots, our strug-gles can breed compassion and our failings forgiveness. As Moses said to his nascent nation, we owe our lives to a God "merciful and gracious, slow to anger, and abounding in steadfast love" (Exodus 34:6).

The Art of Compassion

No one has improved on Henri Nouwen's description of compassion: it "grows with the inner recognition that your neighbor shares your humanity with you. This partnership cuts through all walls which might have kept you separate. Across all barriers of land and language, wealth and poverty, knowledge and ignorance, we are one, created from the same dust, subject to the same laws, destined for the same end."

Nouwen's point is that while we are distinct in the most mundane ways we are alike in the most profound ones. The ways we arbitrarily distinguish ourselves are of little heft compared to the things that make us kin.

You and I may have very different dreams for ourselves, and you may come much closer to realizing yours than I mine, but we both understand what it means to hold a passion for something not yet in our hand and impel ourselves toward it with all our hearts. Your neighbor loses his job or his child her team's Little League game, and even if you've never suffered the same fate you do know what it's like to have your ego bruised, to feel rejected, unwanted, and unworthy, to have confidence eclipsed by doubt, and wonder anxiously about your standing among others. The truth is, each one of us is a rich pastiche of hopes and wishes, fears and uncertainties, aspirations and disappointments. We all want to be treated with respect by strangers, affection by friends, and devotion by family, as Nouwen says, to meet our fellow human beings, with whom we share the weighty burdens of love and hate, life and death.

A story will illustrate my point about compassion. There's a memorable scene in the movie *Five Easy Pieces* where the protagonist, a brash young guy named Bobby, a man of wealth and breeding, goes into a diner with friends, and a waitress refuses to

On Mercy and Punishment

Anthony is a twenty-six-year-old drifter from northern Oregon who could be considered something of a poster child for the war on drugs. A large, imposing man with stooped shoulders and a vacant stare, his rap sheet's littered with a wide array of drug-related arrests for everything from weapons possession, to dealing, to possible involvement in a homicide. Suffice it to say that at face value he's the kind of guy likely to elicit precious little sympathy from a society determined to isolate itself from the degradation and danger he epitomizes. Anthony is a man, as the saying goes, "only his parents could love."

Or could they? When he was four years old Anthony watched his father threaten his mother by holding a gun to her head. When they divorced and his mother struck up a relationship with another man, he had to watch them manufacture methamphetamine in a shed behind their home. At their command, he would bring them sandwiches and drinks. He was forced to sit quietly while they worked, all the while inhaling toxic fumes that were the by-product of their operation. He saw addicts come by the house, buy their meth, and then inject it. He was introduced to the drug himself by his mother's boyfriend.

Anthony was beaten by both his mother and her boyfriend, often with closed fists. He was forced to sleep on the floor of their house, where rodents crawled at night. His father, whom he visited on occasion, later married a woman with an older son, who attempted to molest Anthony. Scratch a little anger, and you'll find a world of pain.

I don't know how long it was between the first time he was a victim of a crime to the first time he was a perpetrator, but I do know he was first arrested when he was nineteen years old. I also know prison represented the first time in his life he could be guaranteed three square meals a day, a bed to sleep on, and health coverage should he take ill.

So what is justice in Anthony's case? Perhaps it is punishment tempered in mercy, judgment deepened in understanding, and sorrow grounded in love. I don't know what I would have become had my parents raised me in this way, nor what my daughter would. There but for the grace of God . . .

The story goes that Jesus scandalized the religious elite by sitting down to dinner with the more scurrilous element from the streets of Capernaum. When he heard their complaints he answered simply, "I desire mercy, and not sacrifice. I came not to call the righteous, but sinners" (Matt. 9:13).

And so I wonder. Were he to come back today, would Jesus dare break bread with Anthony? Would I?

serve him something simple because it's not on the menu. To the pleasure of his companions and the cheers of the audience the arrogant kid wields a razor's edge of sarcastic wit, and uses it to slice the poor woman into ribbons of humiliation for not finding a way to satisfy a simple request.

The director stages the scene in such a way that we're compelled to feel contempt for the waitress's singlemindedness and delight at the rapier way with which Bobby exposes and demeans it, and we do. But with an insight the rest of us lack, the irrepressible writer Studs Terkel once told me how *he* saw the scene, and why he hated it so. It was instructive, but more so, it was profoundly humbling.

"What about the waitress?" Studs fumed in a conversation we had. "What was *her* story? Was it the end of a tough day? How long had she been on her feet? How much abuse had she already taken from other rich, insensitive louts like this guy? Was her boss giving her a hard time? Was he hitting on her? Did she have a sick child at home? Did her husband or boyfriend just up and leave her that morning? Was she earning enough at this crummy little dead-end job to make ends meet, or did her problems follow her home and haunt her at the end of her shift?

"The point is," Terkel said, "we know nothing about her. And neither did he. He had no right to do what he did. What if he just talked to her first, had a two-minute conversation, that's all, found out what kind of a day she'd had, learned where she was coming from? Maybe, just maybe, he'd have thought better of his cruelty."

Think of the story of the good Samaritan in the Gospel of Luke, in which a Jewish man is left stripped and beaten on the side of the road by thieves. He is then ignored by both a priest and a Levite, two supposedly reputable members of society. Only a Samaritan—normally an enemy of the Jews—stops to help the man. In Terkel's eyes the waitress is akin to the beaten man. In my eyes he, Terkel, is the Samaritan himself. Bobby is the thief, and on a bad day, you and I are like the Levite and priest, the ones who paid no mind to a stranger's troubles. While you and I float along unconcerned about the ridicule that's been visited on another human being whose well-being is of no material consequence to us, compassion incarnate happens along in the person of another, a stranger who binds up the man's wounds, gives him food and shelter, and restores his dignity.

The Samaritan knew nothing about this man, so why did he do what he did? I don't know the answer to that question, but I have to wonder if perhaps something in his own past reminded him about what it's like to feel abused and degraded, about violations of his body, about physical and emotional scars that never fully heal. Perhaps he understood how helpless you can feel when you're surrounded by crooks on a dark road or surly customers at a two-bit hash house. Perhaps, as Rabbi Hillel once said, he could look into the face of a stranger and see in that face his brother, his sister, or himself.

That is compassion. It is the recognition that at any given moment some of us are strutting through life and others limping, groping, barely finding our way down that dark road with its thieves and its scoundrels. It is knowing that a few of us are winning our race, a few more are finishing second, and most of us are out of the money. But it is also knowing that we're all trying to make the fullest life we can, and that as we walk by that man lying in the darkened street we can no longer keep walking, for our compassion is his entitlement, and one day his will be ours.

Proud Humility

Legend has it that John Wesley, the founder of Methodism, learned that a British general by the name of James Oglethorpe had caught one of his servants stealing a bottle of wine and beaten him severely for it. Wesley confronted Oglethorpe and asked that the general find it in his heart to forgive the poor servant. "Sir," said the officer, "I *never* forgive." To which Wesley replied, "Then, sir, I hope you never offend!"

An exaggerated sense of one's own goodness is a terrible thing—a fact not lost on Wesley—because it's built on the wobbly premise that I'm inherently better than someone else. Thus the power I have to judge and punish another person's sins outweighs the need I have to confess my own.

Oglethorpe made himself into a demigod; he built himself up by tearing another human being down. He erected a pedestal of loose assumptions and in elevating himself onto that pedestal believed there was a moral distance between himself and the servant. As Wesley implied, he did this because he fancied himself the superior of the two. Whatever combination of foolishness or desperation compelled this poor servant to steal from his master, whatever weakness of will or depravity of conscience he was guilty of, was of no more consequence to the general than was the indubitable fact that he himself had surely succumbed to the temptation of ill-gotten pleasure more than once in his own life. All that mattered was that here was an opportunity to mask his own frailties by castigating another man for his. In the words of the iconoclastic philosopher Alan Watts, no one is more aware of his sinfulness than the saint, because he sees the pride in his humility.

As a friend of mine likes to say, when we sit in judgment of others our heads so swell with misplaced pride that our eyes shut and we are blinded to the magnitude of our failings and the consequence of sin. Or, in the delicate words of Simone Weil, "contact with the sword causes the same defilement, whether it be through the handle or through the point." The line that separates accuser and accused is a slim one indeed.

For all his battlefield heroics, Oglethorpe was at heart a coward because he wouldn't muster the courage to forgive. Make no mistake about it, courage is the one element indispensable to forgiveness, for forgiveness is predicated on our willingness to confront our demons and admit our failures.

I see a bit of the Oglethorpe in myself when I think of some of the social justice work I was involved in at Riverside Church. In keeping with the church's tradition, the issues we tackled—fair housing, racial equality, military disarmament, prison reform, and the like—were laudable. As the saying goes, we were always looking to comfort the afflicted and afflict the comfortable. But the work was risky, because it bred an insidious form of self-righteousness. I far too often allowed the nobility of the cause to

testify to the quality of my character, as though the cause itself
conferred on me some moral superiority over those who were
either antagonistic or indifferent. Rarely did I search my soul to
find where my sins colluded
with theirs. I suppose I did this
because so many of these
issues demanded stridency of
effort and clarity of purpose,
but I also suspect I did it

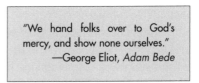

"We hand folks over to God's
mercy, and show none ourselves."
—George Eliot, *Adam Bede*

because I lacked the moral courage to admit the kinship between
us, that though my sins may be of a different nature, they are no
less injurious to others or pernicious to myself.

So it is that in forgiveness we say to another: I don't condone
your actions, and in fact I hold you responsible for them. But in
them I see my own. I look at what you've done and realize that I,
too, could have done this. Like you, I'm justified not by works but
by grace, by love bestowed by God and not earned through mortal
labors, so perhaps there is no greater thing we can share than our
need for confession to override accusation, contrition to outweigh
recrimination, and forgiveness to supersede punishment. Perhaps
our prayer for one another must simply be that the crossing of our
paths might obviate the crossing of our swords.

Confession and forgiveness are like a double helix in this way,
two strands of discrete energy that intertwine because each can't
survive without the other. The strength I need to accept responsibility for my own faults provides me the wisdom to accept the
same inclinations in others. In turn, in their acceptance of me I'm
liberated from the fear that they will condemn me for—in the
words of the Book of Common Prayer—those things left undone
that I ought to have done, and those things done that I ought not to
have done.

I cannot recall how many patients I've treated over the years
whose anxieties were at least worsened, if not initiated, by parents
who lacked the wherewithal to forgive. As one young man eloquently described it: "I would disobey my parents or otherwise do
something wrong, and my father's anger would come at me like a
bursting dam. It washed over everything in sight. But you know

what was worse than that initial onslaught? What was worse was that when the waters subsided, it left behind this sediment, this bitter grit and stench and remembrance that was only added to the next time the dam burst. Layer after layer. Year after year. Maybe that's why I'm here."

I thought of this man not long ago when I was in a friend's house and watched her young child disobey her and break something he wasn't supposed to touch in the first place. The mother chided him, gently but firmly, and the child was duly chastened. Tears fell easily from his eyes, and only when the mother knew her anger had been heard did she take him in her arms, an act of forgiveness. Her expression slowly melted from disappointment to love and his from contrition to wary joy. The storm passed, a few remnants drifted by, but the point was taken and the relationship between the two was, in an odd way, strengthened by what has happened. The boy learned that his actions have consequences, and that he is responsible for them, but he also learned that his mother's love is the constant, the last word, the still point in his turning world, and that he is never in danger of losing it because of any mistakes he makes or any heartache he causes during this very messy process he's going through called childhood. It was a wordless conversation that spoke volumes about the durability of love.

Just as water itself can both wreak havoc like a burst dam and cleanse like a child's tear, our failures and disappointments with one another can serve either to harden the misunderstandings between us or to clarify what it is we must do if, as the psalmist wrote, we are going to live together like brothers and sisters in unity. Failures are not without value, not unredeemable. In the end it is what we do with them—if and how we redeem them—that ultimately determines if they have somehow served a greater purpose.

If it's not a parent and child at odds it is a couple, new lovers or old friends, in-laws or ex-husbands, neighborhoods, or even nations. How many battles might *not* have been waged over the years, how many innocent lives spared and ploughshares beaten into swords, had enemies only sat down together and confessed their less than noble inclinations to one another?

Could Harry Truman and Kim Il Sung have steered us clear of a war that cost the lives of over 2 *million* people (most of whom were civilians) by one admitting his country's interests were imperious and the other that his were geostrategic, and both agreeing that neither showed much interest in the welfare of the people of Korea?

Could Gamal Nasser and Ezer Weizmann have brokered a peace founded on Egypt's confession that it had no right to attack Israel in '67 and Israel's that it had none to reduce the Palestinians to the status of second-class citizens, all in a part of the world billions still call their holy land? I wonder. I wonder how many Israeli and Palestinian children's lives would not have been lost to car bombs, snipers, or strafing helicopters, or if any of those children, given the chance to grow into adulthood, might have discovered a cure for cancer or a remedy for global warming.

I wonder if any of the over eighty conflicts being fought today could be resolved by warring sides admitting that neither one has any moral purchase over the other, and if the 700 billion dollars spent annually on this madness could not better serve humanity by tilling farmland, inoculating babies, housing families, and educating children. I wonder if any nation has the courage to use humility rather than arrogance to resolve its differences with its neighbors.

Just as compassion is grounded in our shared sense of need, forgiveness is grounded in our shared sense of contrition, whether individual or corporate. In forgiveness we come face-to-face with our own failures of will. We accept them, confess them, repent them. We are humbled by them. Only then do we redeem them, and we do this by seeing ourselves in others and extending *to* them the very understanding we want so much to receive *from* them. When forgiveness is requested, offered, accepted, and reciprocated, it becomes like a blossoming field of Easter tulips, fragrant, vivid, life affirming; a contagious force the likes of which relationships, marriages, families, even whole civilizations can be born of and built upon. As Peter Ustinov once said of love, it is an endless act of forgiveness, a tender look that becomes a habit.

On Mercy and Justice

Compassion and forgiveness beg the question of whether mercy reduces us to the disposition of a lamb without the muscle of a lion; whether it boxes us in, ties our hands, and corners us into dismissing the offenses of every unrepentant slumlord, boorish neighbor, racist cop, and tinhorn dictator who ever walked the face of the earth. If we show mercy to the merciless do we countenance the unconscionable, or is it possible to make a stand for justice, hold people answerable for the consequences of their actions, and simultaneously extend to them the same kindness God shows each one of us?

The prophetic voice we hear in our Scriptures is not only compatible with mercy but predicated on it, because mercy is nothing if not finding our own pain mirrored in the pain of a fallen world to the point where the two become indistinguishable. We know from our own lives that compassion relieves suffering and confession forgives sin, and we know too that this is the world's need as well. Like the good Samaritan, we are to love the wounded by coaxing her back to wholeness and the thief by calling him back to repentance, and we do so out of a profound understanding of our own need for both. We also hold the powers that be accountable to make the roads safer. James reminds us that it profits us nothing if we have faith but not works (James 2:14), and Paul that even if we give up everything we own but have not love we gain nothing (1 Corinthians 13:3)—all of which is another way of saying that while mercy without action is pity and action without mercy condescension, when we wed the two together we have a formidable basis for biblical justice. As Shakespeare wrote, "mercy seasons justice."

So it is that our faith beseeches us to find a way to engage that struggle anywhere in the world that is bereft of mercy, be it in our home, our neighborhood, another city, or in far-flung places we have never even been before. From Mexico's sweltering *malquiadoras* to China's underground churches, from America's overcrowded prisons to Rwanda's overtaxed refugee camps, whether with our time, our resources, our prayers, or our votes, it is our sacred responsibility to call the oppressed to courage and the oppressors to account, because at heart neither one is a stranger to us. As Jesus warns later in Matthew's Gospel, stand tall against the religious hypocrites who "tithe mint and dill and cumin and neglect the weightier matters of the law, justice, mercy, and faith" (23:23).

An eloquent passage speaks to this point in John Steinbeck's classic novel *The Grapes of Wrath*. In his quest to find work in California, young Tom Joad, a depression-era Oklahoma dust bowler whose family farm the wind has literally blown away, is musing on the many difficulties he has endured in his travels, how hard his life has become, and the impunity with which people who have power wield it over people who don't. With a resoluteness that is the residue of the cruelty he's endured, Tom promises his mother,

> Wherever there's a fight so hungry people can eat, I'll be there. Wherever there's a cop beatin' up a guy, I'll be there. I'll be there in the way guys yell when they're mad. I'll be there in the way kids laugh when they're hungry and they know supper's ready. An' when the people are eatin' the stuff they raise, and livin' in the houses they build, I'll be there, too.

When I think of Tom I think of the beaten man whom the Samaritan rescued. I'd like to believe the kindness that was extended to him was not lost on him, that he was forever changed by it, and that hereafter he would walk the roads of his life vigilant not only to the dangers that threatened him but to the souls who saved him and the victims who need him. That he would *be* there, so much so that he would even forgive those who passed him by.

Should he have done this he would have fulfilled this beatitude. By teaching us that the merciful will receive mercy Jesus is saying that mercy is at heart not just a gesture of goodwill—this is half of it—but a reciprocal action, a relationship of give and take, generosity and gratitude, each rooted in the other. Blessed mercy is neither discourse nor soliloquy. It is, as Terkel said, conversation.

Sanctification: Blessed Are the Pure in Heart

Before I write something, I wash my hands. I always want to say I approached [my work] with clean hands—you know, a symbolic cleansing.
—August Wilson

Each beatitude demands something of us except this one—it demands everything. In the long reach of human history, since first being turned away from the garden, the whole of our endeavor has been to return to God, to see the face we hid from in shame and disobedience, to reclaim our innocence, or at least some shred of it.

But I believe we find it difficult to think of purity as something to aspire to, let alone attain. So easy is it when we are down to believe that within every silver lining there lurks a dark cloud, and that no good deed goes unpunished. Anne Frank wrote from her hiding place that despite the horrors of war she still believed people were good at heart; but we have our doubts, and we wonder if she continued to believe it after the Nazis found her out and marched her family off to the camps. I watch a young man approach an old woman in a subway station and offer to carry her groceries up the long flight of stairs, and my first thought is that when he hits the top he will march off with them as well. Apparently it is hers, too. She politely turns him down, and bears her burden alone.

It is almost reflexive to question the motive behind a kind gesture or the sincerity behind a good intention, and we often do. We sometimes live in wary distance from one another, unconvinced that purity is anything more than the quaint coin of the infant's realm, a childish thing to be outgrown, the way a little girl outgrows her first dress. Communities are gated, airports guarded, cars alarmed, and children fingerprinted. (We have more guns per capita than any other industrialized nation; one out of every six households where a child lives has at least one.) We don't welcome our distance from others; indeed we do everything in our power to convince them of our sincerity and good faith, but our natural inclination is to believe more in our own trustworthiness than theirs. We are as far away now as humanity ever has been from that single cosmic moment, the last moment of pure innocence, the moment just *before* the serpent made Eve curious and God furious. With this as a backdrop, what is it that Jesus asks of us, and why?

The Inevitability of God

When in Psalm 24 David asks rhetorically who will enter the temple and receive God's blessing, he answers his own question with the words, "Those who have clean hands and a pure heart," and this is Jesus' point of reference here. It is an observation at one and the same time both obvious and discreet; obvious because holy space is never to be entered into disrespectfully, and discreet because in this psalm the temple is not so much a building as a state of mind. "The earth is the Lord's and all that is in it," the psalm begins, which is to say, *all* of God's creation is holy, is the divine dwelling place, is sacred ground, and so is to be entered in purity of heart and cleanliness of hands. As the English journalist Malcolm Muggeridge observed while visiting the Sisters of Charity in Calcutta, either life is always sacred or it is intrinsically of no account; it cannot be both.

In all that we experience, from the most terrible to the most beautiful, there is the potential for God to be made known to us. As Paul Tillich stated, God can be revealed through sacred texts or holy lives, liturgy or prayer. Or for that matter, he said, through a stick or a stone.

When we are attentive to the divine we may from time to time steal little glimpses of it, wafting wisps suffusing the everyday. I remember a nun I once knew who described what she called "the sanctity of her morning coffee" in this way: "I arise in silence, come into the kitchen, take up the bag of coffee, and let the aroma drift into the air. After I measure it, I go to the sink to pour my water. I look out the window at the dawning day, to the dewy grass, the hibiscus bush in my yard, and the occasional starling nesting under the eaves of the house. When the coffee is brewed, I pour it, and then sit for a moment at the kitchen table, both hands wrapped around the cup, the warmth penetrating my hands and taking away the morning's chill. Then I put the cup to my lips and take my first steaming sip. It is a ritual I have, this morning coffee. It is comforting, solitary, peaceful, and so, in a strange way, it is something of a prayerful experience. I am ready to start my day, 'at work,' as they say, 'in the field of the Lord.'" A holy moment, refreshing as the morning dew and inviting as a quiet curl of lazy steam.

As Annie Dillard observed in *For the Time Being,* "God shows an edge of himself to souls who seek him, and the people who bear those souls, marveling, know it, and see the skies carousing around them, and watch cells stream and multiply in green leaves." And, we might add, prayers waft heavenward in ascendant vapor.

I once observed a schoolteacher working with her young students to find God in the green leaves in a park near my home. She trotted them off to a wooded area and asked each one to pick up four twigs and create a small "corral" with them on the ground. She then had them just sit patiently and watch. "Look inside your corral and see what kind of life you can find there," she told them. "Take your time. Look at the bugs, or the grass, or the rocks, or the scraps of bark. Imagine what might live beneath the ground. Let's see how much life there is in even the smallest corner of creation."

It was a wonderful exercise, because as the children paid close attention their eyes were slowly opened to this extraordinary bouquet of creative energy—so many different expressions of the very same life force—emanating out of their own tiny patch of dirt. I came away thinking that with a little luck these kids would forever see their own fields of the Lord in a whole new way. God revealed, through a stick or a stone.

But sticks and stones can hurt as well. Just as we can find the sacred in the profane, so too can we make a sacrilege of even our holiest of things, such as prayers for victory by athletes in the race or zealots in the Holy War. Some years ago I had a conversation with a Roman Catholic priest by the name of George Zabelka. In August of 1945 George served as the military chaplain who was responsible for giving his blessing to the crew and mission of the *Enola Gay,* the plane that dropped the atomic bomb on Hiroshima. "I believed I was doing God's work," George told me, "but now, when I look at the enormous evil that bomb unleashed I realize I was terribly, terribly wrong. When I think of myself standing over that plane in my priestly vestments I cannot help but think: 'So this is what it means to be a wolf in sheep's clothing.'"

When decisions determine faith rather than vice versa we engage in the basest form of idolatry, because we create a God whose image is nothing more than the extension of our own prejudice. This is why both Jesus and the psalmist urge us to that most elusive task, the purification of our hearts, for it is absolutely foundational to our ability to discern the face of God in our world. To be truly faithful is to come to God asking that our beliefs and actions be informed rather than simply endorsed. Or, as Kierkegaard wrote, purity of heart means to will one thing.

Purity of Heart, Purity of Intention

The legend of the Holy Grail has it that one day Sir Launfal rode off determined to find the Grail, the cup Jesus used at the Last Supper. On his way out of the city, he came upon a beggar who was desperate for a little money so that he might eat. Launfal, knowing what the church expected of him but at the same time filled with derision for this lowly man, sneered at him, looked with contempt, and, while still on his horse, tossed a few gold coins at the beggar's feet. Despite his ravenous hunger, the beggar knew himself to be a human being, loved in the eyes of God. He refused the money. Launfal went on his way, devoting years of his life in the pursuit of the Grail he never found.

Captivating Freedom

There may be nothing more difficult in all the world than to come to God pure and unalloyed, so suffused are we with things that distract us from being fully present to a God who waits to be revealed in all that is around us. As Dorothy Soelle has observed, purity of heart is as strange to us as the wind to the slack kite. We want to be open, to let God's breath lift our souls the way the wind would lift that kite, but urges and anxieties often hold us down.

"Do not be anxious about your life," Jesus tells us a little later in the sermon, "about what you will eat or drink or wear," because none of them have ever added so much as one moment to a person's existence. But we are anxious about all sorts of things, and by this I don't mean the anxiety that is the manifestation of every parent's love for their child and prayer for their safety and happiness. We worry about whether we'll get that report finished on time. Will the car hold up through another winter? Are my parents going to get divorced? Will my child stay away from drugs? To paraphrase Shel Silverstein's whimsical, poignant poem "WHATIF," "whatif" the bus is late, my teeth don't grow in straight, I tear my pants, or never learn to dance?

There is a story of an old man who, on his deathbed, was asked if he had any regrets. "Only one," he answered. "I only wish I had all the time back I spent worrying about bad things that never happened." The all-consuming whatifs.

Anxious moments are impure moments because in them we are not disposed to God, not listening to God's assurance that things will play out as they must, and that God will help us with all of our whatifs. Instead we are consumed with precisely the things that Jesus—a man who never had a steady job or a roof over his head, who never knew where his next meal was coming from or when he would be arrested for the courage of his convictions—has told us to let go of. Purity of heart means lightening our psychological and emotional loads; remember Kris Kristofferson's (popularized by Janis Joplin) definition of freedom—"nothin' left to lose."

If it is not anxiety that keeps us from being fully present to God, it is some other human thrust, just as banal, just as trite, something as unnecessary as it is compelling. Maybe there is someone in our life we are angry with in that stubborn, foolish way that lingers because cowardice masquerades as principle and we refuse to relent when all we really want is to put the whole mess behind us. "So if you are offering your gift at the altar and there remember that your brother has something against you," Jesus instructs a little later in the sermon, "leave your gift there before the altar and go, be first reconciled to your brother, and then come and offer your gift" (Matt. 5:24). We cannot be of two minds when offering ourselves to God.

If not this, perhaps it's lust or jealousy, prejudice or greed, ill-bred confidence or unfounded fear that keeps our hearts from purity and our minds from God. There is a story of two Buddhists, a teacher and his student, walking through the woods one day. They come upon a river, and on the bank is a woman who can't get across but wants to. The teacher picks her up, carries her across, and puts her down. The two go on their way. Miles go by. After hours of mental torture, the student turns to the teacher and says, "I can't stand this anymore! I have to ask you—back there at the river, you picked up that woman, and yet we are forbidden to touch women!" The teacher looked kindly at his student, paused for a moment, and said, "Yes, I picked her up. And I carried her across. And I put her down. You, on the other hand, are still carrying her." Whatever it is that burdens your heart, that corrupts its purity, put it down.

A Slice of Heaven

As I pointed out earlier, when the Hebrews were exiled from their homeland by the Babylonians they were very much adrift in the wilderness. They had no home, no nation, no temple. Their community was in pieces, scattered across the Near East like the bits of a sandcastle taken back to the sea by the tide. In order to preserve their sense of identity as Jews, to bind them to one another and to keep them mindful of God, they put special emphasis on their unique rituals of purity and cleanliness—circumcision, family cleanliness, kosher laws, and the like. They did this assiduously because it was a way of remembering who they were in God's eyes despite being strangers in foreign and sometimes hostile lands.

When we consider our own exile, that sense of feeling torn between the demands and enticements of the world around us and the glint of the God who is its creator—a God deeply felt but maddeningly unseen—we look for ways to quiet that world and draw closer to its sustenance and source.

We say a blessing before a meal and the bread on our plate becomes sacramental, a gift, for which we are grateful—a slice of heaven. We begin or end our day in silent contemplation of a line from a favorite psalm or poem, perhaps Psalm 25: "Relieve the troubles of my heart," or T. S. Eliot: "Teach us to care and not to care; teach us to sit still." Such things can provide the keys to the morning and the lock upon the night. Deeply observant Jews will treat their Sabbath with such respect that they will not drive a car, or light a light, or run an errand, or do any such thing that will remove them from the holiness of the day. Instead they spend it solely with one another, celebrating the unique joys and burdens of chosenness, and restoring them for the week ahead.

A piece of food, food for thought, the sustenance of a day of rest. Ordinary things turned into ordinary miracles, windows to the divine. We cleanse ourselves of all anxious and unworthy thoughts and give ourselves to God.

Purity of heart is a profoundly interior experience; it is the bliss that attends when we hoist the weight of our worries from our shoulders and commune in blessed simplicity with a God whose only concern is that we have none, who lifts our kite and lets it soar to the skies, unencumbered by the tug of baser impulses.

Such flight is no small thing in and of itself, for of what use is a faith that does not liberate us but leaves us captive to those impulses? With purity of heart comes the knowledge that God is never far from us, and that when we enter into a space in a pure way it becomes holy. It could be a meal or a marriage, a worship service, a passing conversation, or an outing with our children. When free from the jealousies, hurts, angers, and anxieties that are our frequent companions and impediments, we are free to love and be loved by God.

Even in those times when our hearts are made heavy and our demons are getting the better of us, if just once in our lives we've experienced purity of heart, that in itself is worth something, because it serves to remind us—much like bread and wine remind us of our Savior's sacrifice—of something wonderful, experienced long ago, but no less real despite how out of reach it seems today. There is a story of a group of little children in London, orphaned during the Second World War. The children had a terrible time trying to sleep, so afraid they were that they would wake up and be left alone again, with no one at the orphanage or anywhere else in the city to take care of them. One of the guardians, seeing this, decided one night to give each child a piece of bread to sleep with. "Let this remind you," she told them, "that for all of the uncertainties, we fed you today, and we will be here to feed you tomorrow." With that, the children slept through the night.

But as the psalmist reminds us, although purity of heart gives us passage to God, there is more to it than an interior experience alone. Who, he asks, will *see* God? "Those who have *clean hands* and a pure heart." Clean hands: the tools of our labors, labors of love. We live in an impure world, and if we let God go into our heart but not then emerge from it we allow comfort to snuff out discipleship. God expects our thoughts to be pure, and our actions to be clean as well. We give our cloak when our coat is asked for, walk a second mile when one will do, turn the other cheek when the first one is slapped.

We build the temple that this psalm speaks of and we do so with our very hands. We lift and strain and sweat with one another, work beside our neighbor and together place one great timber beside the next. Slowly, and over time, the temple begins to take shape. It is a new school in rural Texas, a community center for the elderly in suburban Detroit, affordable housing in New York City. It is a water filtration plant in Senegal, a union headquarters in Nicaragua, a rebuilt hospital in Bosnia.

Clean hands are what a father uses to embrace his prodigal child now come home. They are two brothers, long feuding, who reach out to one another in mutual forgiveness and rapprochement. They are the blessing of a benediction, the integrity of a day's work, a friendly wave to a lonely stranger on a park bench.

"And there was a leper," Matthew writes, "who came down to him and knelt before him." Jesus "stretched out his hand, and touched him" (Matt. 8:2). And healed him. He did not waste any time; this was the very first thing Jesus did after preaching the sermon. Clean hands: hands at work, hands that heal the sick, caress the lonely, uplift the destitute, build the kingdom.

Some years ago I was part of a consortium of clergy in Harlem whose charge was to rebuild old and rundown housing. We held our meetings in a small church near a dilapidated building in the poorest section of New York City. The median income was just over six thousand dollars. One day when I was on my way into the church a woman called out to me from a stoop across the street. She looked tired but proud, old beyond her years but with plenty of fight left in her. She wore a threadbare housecoat and mismatched shoes, but sat upright and dignified.

"When are we gonna build me a home?" she yelled to me. I liked her choice of words; she didn't want us to do it for her, but with her.

"I honestly don't know," I told her, "but Lord, I hope it's soon."

"Not as much as I do," she answered.

Some months later I went back for another meeting, and out in front of her stoop was a pile of lumber and a palette of cinder blocks. We were going to build her home. I didn't see her, but I had to wonder what she thought when she saw the building materials.

A pile of lumber and a palette of cinder blocks, I thought to myself. Sticks and stones. The face of God. Together, she and I, the churches in the community, the will of the people, the faith of a city, the wisdom of the elders, were going to join together and build this woman her temple. Clean hands and pure hearts. When it was done, she would, as the psalmist wrote, "ascend the hill of the Lord . . . and stand in his holy place." We are God's hands on earth.

To Wonder and to Act

Saint Gregory Thaumaturgus advised us to wonder intelligently. Behold the glory of what God has done, and then know, in turn, what you must do with it. Contemplate the bounty of the heavens and pledge yourself to the beauty of the earth. Heart and hand, soul and strength in symmetry with one another, this is the very core of what it means to live the life of faithful discipleship, for when we cherish God's love for us but refuse to actively love others we are like the straw Pharisee who later in this Gospel sees Jesus healing a man whose hand has withered but wonders only whether the healing action is in violation of Sabbath law. By the same logic, if we immerse ourselves in the labors of the world but in a way that cuts us off from the God who is the very ground of our being, we run the risk of becoming spiritually exhausted, world weary, depleted, impure, perhaps even cynical.

These two pieces, each indispensable to the other, together form a whole that is itself the indispensable life of faith. They cannot survive isolated from one another any more than a tree can survive without the soil or the sun, but together they forge a mighty bond with roots in the earth and wings toward the sky that has been known to part seas, move mountains, and raise the dead.

The Purity of Simply Trying

If we could live all our days, and all our moments in those days, in the condition that this beatitude calls us to, we'd have little need for the other seven. We would be at home with the pure, perfect wisdom Plato spoke of in *The Republic* as the highest ideal to which any human being could possibly attain. We would be fully secure in our place in God's kingdom and unequivocally committed to contributing to its continuing emergence. We would out-saint the saints.

But life is not lived at home, and even Plato's wisdom was a strain to touch, let alone to hold. No, purity is not a thing to attain, but nor is it simply the fiction of our noblest dreams, a perfection easy to mythologize and impossible to materialize. I do not believe it is within our power to live in a state of pure heart and clean hands, but I do believe we can, from time to time and when serendipity cooperates, get a taste of it.

But as I've said elsewhere, our lives mitigate against purity, just as all human lives always have. Errands need to be run, noses wiped, meals put on the table, parking spaces quibbled over. We are, each one of us, a constant tangle of competing desires and demands, pulling us ever deeper into our faith one moment and farther away the next. One day all's right with the world and the next a close relative receives bad news in an X ray, but at the very least she has a family who will care for her. A stirring Christmas service rekindles our hope for peace on earth, and then three days later there is a car bombing in Tel Aviv or a flood in Calcutta. But three days after that there is an outpouring of generosity for the victims the likes of which would lift the spirits of even the most ardent skeptics. Today's pat on the back becomes tomorrow's pink slip, and just as we begin to wonder if God can really be bothered with such trivialities as ours, with luck and persistence, another job might come our way. Our parade is rained on, but still we march, not because we believe one day the sun will shine forever, but because at various points in our lives we have been afforded enough of a glimpse of the divine, enough of a taste of purity of heart, to know that even when all isn't right, God is. We will always experience times when we feel far from God (what the philosopher Pascal called the God-shaped void in our heart) but that doesn't mean that God is far from us.

It is because purity is such a fragile, fleeting thing that we must latch on to symbols of it, markers that point us to it and remind us that there is a God to be seen. This is what artists, at their best, do for us. Like a flash of light in a freeze frame, they seize and immortalize the moment and turn it over to us. Perhaps it's the understated strength of a Georgia O'Keeffe watercolor, the overwhelming power of a Jacques Lipschutz sculpture, or a child's fingerpainted rendering of her family, hung proudly on the refrigerator door. Or maybe it's the apocalyptic haunt of a Bob Dylan ballad that reminds us of God's immanence, or perhaps a Mozart Kyrie or a Gregorian chant. But whatever the vehicle the effect is the same: the imponderable pure becomes real when it is symbolically shaped by human hands in contours that match perfectly the void within us.

Wholeness: Blessed Are the Peacemakers

We will not have peace by afterthought.
—Norman Cousins

We do not desire peace, nor should we. We don't desire it any more than we desire the air we breathe or the food we eat. Peace is not an ancillary thing but a fundament; not a stem but a root; not the embroidery that makes a pleasant life more meaningful or a hard one more bearable. No, peace is the center, the core, the one thing capable of making whole that which is fractious, resonant that which is hollow, becalmed that which is tempestuous, meaningful that which is absurd. It is what holds us together when forces within and without threaten to rip us apart. Said the illustrious Rabbi Hillel, a near contemporary of Jesus whose preaching, like Jesus', dug into the very core of Judaism, "Be of the disciples of Aaron, loving peace and pursuing it."

Indeed, it was the absence of this peace that explained to me why a patient of mine whom I will call Jack, a fit, twenty-something, Ivy League–educated executive, so rich in things but poor in soul, with the world at his feet, tailored clothes on his back, and pricey trinkets in his toy box, wondered aloud where his dogged feelings of sadness come from. "I can't just go into a store and buy peace of mind like I buy everything else," he tells me sadly. This is what Rabbi Eugene Borowitz once called "air-conditioned unhappiness." Who am I to disagree?

But it's also peace's promise that explained to me why a long-time friend, a wizened old country pastor, privy as she was to the quiet storms that stirred throughout her congregation—the shaky marriage in the first pew, the petulant child in the second, the wayward temptations of the fellow in the back—could still greet them each and every Sunday with those durable, timeworn, and heartfelt words from the apostle Paul, "The peace of God be with you." Declaring peace where it is in scarce supply, she knows, does not strain credulity, it nurtures believability. Which is why they would answer her, "And also with you."

What is it if not the prostitution of peace that allows kings and queens, presidents and prime ministers, insurrectionists and warlords, to justify their machinations of war; as if the world's salvation can only be ensured by the threat of its destruction? Armies of God, Holy Crusades, Peacekeeper Missiles, Onward Christian Soldiers . . . when we vitiate the purity of peace with the poison of war we forget at our peril the words of the psalmist: "the warhorse is a vain hope for victory, and by its great might it cannot save."

So what is this thing we so often chase after the way a child chases after a flittery lightning bug on a warm June evening? Why is it so skittish, so elusive? And why, when with a little luck and a touch of persistence we *do* catch it, secrete it away in our little jar, and clamp the lid down tight, does the light, once captured, not glow forever?

Peace Is Not Partial

Shalom: the eternal verity, the poet's muse, the prophet's grail, the lover's glint, the pilgrim's lighted trail. A word so rich in meaning, it loses a little something of itself in its mere utterance, as though no set of letters, however artfully strung together or reverently spoken, is ever capable of adequately conveying the power of the ideal that lies behind them. Like René Magritte's painting of a pipe that he entitled "Ceci n'est pas un pipe" ("This Is Not a Pipe"; it wasn't; it was a *representation* of a pipe), our words are at best loose approximations, arrows pointing to the thing, rather than the thing itself. The peace of God, as Paul wrote, passes all understanding.

To speak of peace is to speak of completeness, proportion, and balance. In the words of Emily Dickinson, it is "to comprehend the whole." Peace is the Zen paradox whereby we can lack everything and still want for nothing, because wholeness is not a function of meeting our desires but of releasing ourselves from their power. To be at peace is to translate something of the purity of God's nature into human terms. Peace upholds the covenant and our fealty to it, releases us from the anxiety we feel when doubt intrudes upon faith so much so that we question whether God is truly there to love and guide us through life. In peace the veil of unknowing is lifted.

"Peace I leave with you, my peace I give to you," Jesus told his followers in the Gospel according to John (14:27). God's emissary, death crossing his path like the lengthening shadow of a late day, assures his disciples that there is no need to worry about anything, no circumstance so dire or burden so large, no challenge so weighty or need so great, that God's love will be in any way compromised by it. "Peace I leave with you, my peace I give to you." It is there for the taking, God in our midst, ready to assure us that whatever our battle, we do not wage it alone. If we are not going to know comfort here, we are not going to know it anywhere. But then, if we do find it here, we will need look no further.

But why must we look at all? Why doesn't it just come and light upon our shoulder when we take our first breath and remain our constant companion until we take our last?

I do not believe it is necessarily in our nature, let alone our culture, let alone *any* culture, to hold fast and firm to the things of peace. Think back to the story of the garden of Eden, a wonderfully symbolic tale of how what God wants for us is so often at odds with what we want for ourselves. Perhaps you can see the garden as God's promise that we will be cared for, the tree of knowledge as the boundaries that separate us from the immortals, and the sweetness of its fruit as our innate desire to override those boundaries. Perhaps Adam and Eve are every one of us at those times when it's harder to be grateful for what has been given to us than itchy for what's been kept from us.

Whether that itch is a sin or merely an annoyance depends on who's scratching and why; a megalomaniac hungers for power, a social climber for status, a celebrity for fame, an inveterate adulterer for another's spouse, and in each of these almost cartoonishly ego-driven passions it's not hard to catch the fetor of hubris, greed, vanity, or lust. These are people who don't want so much to nibble the fruit as to devour the tree. But though our own rumbling of discord may surface in a far more modest way—less a tabloid headline than a restless night or an unbidden tear—it is discord all the same.

So perhaps for us it's a house that's too small for our family or a school that's too large for our kids. Perhaps it's an old colleague who has forgotten our fortieth birthday, or a new one who has forgotten our name. Maybe it's the promotion we didn't get, or the illness we did, the child out past curfew or the cigarette pack we found in his coat pocket, the middle-age regret over challenges we failed to take, people we refused to love, milestones we could never reach, millstones we could never loose, or slights we could never forgive. Unmet needs all, some petty and some rather just, some that we are right to want to satisfy and others simply wise to accept. But that's not the point, really, for it ultimately doesn't matter if we are of high society or low estate, or whether the fruit we seek is close to the ground or well up into the heart of the tree. The point is well made in the Bhagavad Gita, where it is written that only one who knows peace has forgotten desire.

I remember a conversation about inner peace I once had with a wonderful old monk by the name of Brother Jeremy, a holy man who lived in a monastery in central Michigan and who was quite committed to this solitary way of life. "What do you think we talk about, my brothers and I?" he once asked me.

"I don't know," I answered. "I guess I always figured you guys hit on the big-ticket items—y'know, God and the presence of evil, the writings of the church fathers, the theology of the resurrection, that sort of thing."

"Well, yes," he answered patiently, "we do. But we also talk about other things. Walk around the grounds long enough and you're likely to hear one of us say to another, 'Well, I see I'm back on kitchen detail *again* next week.' Or 'Did you ever notice how often Brother James is allowed to drive into town?' Or maybe,

'Brother Dominick's cell is next to mine. He snores.' The point is, we don't simply 'attain' peace forever and at all times. If we're lucky, we're aware of those occasions when it invites us out onto the dance floor, whisks us across the room, and, for a while anyway, holds us as if we are one."

Brother Jeremy's was a wonderful point, well taken; even the holiest of men and women—people whose very vocation is to plumb the depths of their spiritual wells—must contend with the turbulence of everyday living, of bumping into one another, stepping on one another's toes, getting their feelings hurt or their hopes dashed, and otherwise muddling through as best they can.

So whether by the clumsiness of our hand or the conspiracy of our fate, the constraints of our very human nature or the whims of nature itself, peace is in this way both alluring and elusive, the light in the darkness, darting and dancing, soaring and seducing, begging us hither to that place that passes all understanding, only to then flit away and land again elsewhere, always seemingly elsewhere, on another's shoulder. Even there, it is only to again take wing.

Speaking Peace in a World of Conflict

But in truth peace *does* present itself. We have all had those moments when preparation meets opportunity; when we are open to receive peace and the world around us is open to bestow it; when our troubles and strivings don't so much disappear as dissipate, like a clenched fist that slowly loosens. When this happens we are

One of the sweetest examples of peace in the face of vicissitude is a story told of St. Francis of Assisi, an ascetic monk of great simplicity who believed that when we are close to beauty we are close to God. When one day a visitor found Francis out in his garden, hoeing, the visitor asked him, "Francis, what if you were to learn that the world were to come to a calamitous end tomorrow? What would you do?" After pausing a moment, Francis looked at the visitor, smiled, and said, "I'd keep hoeing."

overwhelmed by that sweet sense of calm, of knowing that at this moment in our life there is no urge to be somewhere else or someone else. We know that no unmet desire is preoccupying us, no gnawing "if only . . ." niggling away at our contentment, no problem that cannot—with God's help and our own—be nursed to its completion.

Peace is serenity; it is that inner place we tiptoe to every so often where there is nothing we must change in the present, regret in the past, or dread in the future. It is not necessarily a state of perfection but it *is* a perfect acceptance of our life as it is being lived at that moment. To paraphrase Thich Nhat Hanh, the miracle isn't walking on water but walking on the earth, fully alive to every moment. So the kids may be fighting and the milk may have gone bad, but in peace we trust that nothing cataclysmic will come of it; that in time children tire themselves out, another carton of milk can be opened, and the steady beating pulse of mother earth will not have missed a beat. As Marcel Proust wrote in *Remembrance of Things Past:*

> We do not succeed in changing things according to our desire, but gradually our desire changes. The situation that we hoped to change because it was intolerable becomes unimportant. We have not managed to surmount the obstacle, as we were absolutely determined to do, but life has taken us round it, led us past it, and then if we turn round to gaze at the remote past, we can barely catch sight of it, so imperceptible has it become.

But it is more than serenity or acceptance. It is proportion too. I remember some of my days in church ministry when I would put in long hours at work, busier than thou, and think myself quite the giving one, tending to the needs of this congregant or that task force, planning the next baptism, potluck supper, or protest. The work I was doing had merit, but as often as not I think it was the pleasure I derived from saying to myself: "Well, they really need you, don't they? Aren't *you* important!" that compelled me. I needed the activity to convince myself of my own worthiness, which is another way of saying that on some level I felt terribly unsure of myself. But in peace we have no shortcomings to compensate for and no subterranean miseries to sublimate. We don't overindulge with food or drink or work or play, are not unduly driven by old ghosts, don't punish ourselves with deprivation, distract ourselves with material luxury, or inflate ourselves with false pride. Our wants are few and our needs managed, and, like a Vermeer painting, each moment radiates with the soft light of quiet gratitude that rises heavenward in thanks to God.

But it is more still, because it also includes trust, knowing, as a friend of mine once said, "if not what the future holds, then at least who holds the future." In peace we do not so much believe in the power of God's love to guide our lives—the way we would believe, say, that planting a bag of seeds will yield a bed of flowers—as we do behold it, feel it, experience it, the way we experience the flowers themselves. In the words of Hannah Arendt, "nothing we use or hear or touch can be expressed in words that equal what is given by the senses." In the end, the trust that peace engenders is a sensual thing, a thing to be physically experienced, intoxicating with fragrance, soothing to the touch, pleasing on the eyes, humbling in its magnificence.

But even this is not enough, because when we are at peace we are at service to God, as ours is a reflection of the divine peace. I believe this is what Jesus means a little later in the Sermon on the Mount when he tells his followers: "let your light so shine before others so that they may see your good works and give glory to your Father in heaven" (Matthew 5:16). It is this peace that God has given us, left with us, that we uphold as a kind of quiet testament, the lightning bug in the dead of night; it does not blind the world around it but breaks through the darkness nonetheless to remind any and all who behold its little glow that God is watching over us, and that we need not be afraid.

What this bears witness to is the responsibility that comes with being at peace, because to let that light so shine means to live peaceably with others under circumstances that are not always easy. As a rabbi friend of mine once put it, "Unfortunately, in speaking of peace, when all is said and done, more is said than done." It's one thing to talk about it, quite another to actualize it in a resistant world. Peace is kept when we refuse to break it and strife is broken when we refuse to answer it. In peace we do as God does by loving others impartially. In impassioned peace we exercise the moral thrust of active love, for what less than active love grounded in peace converted Zacchaeus into a champion of the poor and the working class, the two Marys—Magdalene and the mother of Jesus—into humble servants and the last ones to leave the cross and the first to bind the wounds? What less than this could have made Mahatma Gandhi refuse to eat, Rosa Parks refuse to move, or Nelson Mandela refuse to capitulate, each one doing so in the name of felling an institution of hegemony and hatred? As the Dalai Lama once put it, world peace begins with inner peace.

So what, in the end, are the things of peace? They are the sense of wholeness that comes in knowing that the love of God that is poured out for us is durable and enduring; the balance we strike between the competing claims upon our life, our time, our values, and our affections; the restraint we exercise over the impulses of our lower angels, and the calm determination with which we exercise it. They are the satisfaction and gratitude that come in discerning the ways we can bring it to bear in the lives of others.

But it's not peace that Jesus is blessing in this beatitude but peace*makers,* which is to say, peace is really the product of human effort. For the child to catch lightning in a jar he must first find his way to the meadow in the dead of night, give himself over to the task, remain alert, quiet, still, patient, and in every other way inviting; he must give his whole self, body and soul, over to the process. Peace does not come where it does not feel invited or stay where it does not feel welcomed. The child must stand reverently, hands cupped, open, as if a supplicant receiving a sacrament. Then and only then might it come.

When I think of all it takes to be disposed to peace I think of how difficult Brother Jeremy found it to live in peace even within the confines of a cloistered community steeped in faith and conviction. The slope is much steeper for the rest of us, I think, living as we do in a world that lacks even the artifice of protection that the monastery walls offer, shares no common pledge or covenant, and is often at cross-purposes with itself.

I sit in the park near my home and revel at the innocence of children at play, only to have one taunt another unmercifully because her clothes are shabby, or her parents worship the wrong god, or live in the wrong neighborhood. I wonder how, if we can't teach our kids to be more generous toward one another, they will ever grow to be generous adults. Or I lie awake at night ostensibly asking God to grant me peace but really—in my heart of hearts—trying to dictate its terms, ignoring Harry Emerson Fosdick's sage advice that in maturity of prayer we stop asking God to "give us . . ." and instead ask him only to "change us. . . ." The next morning I promise to do better, to be at peace with anyone I encounter that day, but quickly renege when I spot the guy with twelve items at the supermarket's "ten only" checkout. Then I feel ashamed, petty, and not a little embarrassed at my petulance over something so small and stupid. Whether bridled by a reluctant conscience, a fear to change, or simply the childish impulse to satisfy my own desires at the expense of others, I find the making of peace truly one of the most daunting tasks.

Which isn't to say it's impossible; it's just not reflexive. We must, as the child in the meadow, anticipate, prepare, and assume a disposition that allows for peace. Those who have gotten a good grip on this understand the difference between reaction and response, understand that as we are beset by things less likely to enhance our peace than disturb it we do well to consciously resist the natural impulse to answer in kind. Thus when Jesus exhorts us to turn the other cheek he is not so naïve as to think it doesn't hurt to have the first one slapped, or that rage doesn't impinge on us, doesn't well up inside us and want to burst forth like fireworks on the Fourth of July. He's saying that in meeting evil with evil we ultimately do ourselves harm, feeding a spiral of vitriol that could begin with mere annoyance but end with pure hatred. If instead we let the pain or indignation into us but are not absorbed by it, feel our anger rise only to feel it then fall again, understand that, in the words of the old African adage, a finger pointed in accusation at another is three fingers pointed at ourselves, then we accomplish two things. First, in discovering the power of peace to defuse an incendiary situation we strengthen our resolve to live within its blessings. Second, in refusing to lower ourselves to another's behavior by rising to their bait we cannot help but serve as a witness to them as well, that in peace there is the power to overcome the twin demons of aggression and retaliation.

I am reminded of a story told to me by Carl Andreas, a man of sharp mind and clear wit, a serious Mennonite who knew how to be devout without being insufferable. Carl was living in Detroit in the mid-1960s when, after years of hostility and mistrust, a race riot—a revolt, really—broke out in the inner city and threatened to engulf the entire region in flames and bloodshed. A few days into the disturbances there was no sign of the tensions easing, and in fact crimes against property and humanity steadily, ominously rose. The city was falling apart. People were angry, frightened, suspicious of those who they once called their neighbors. Gunshots were commonplace and children were kept inside for fear of their very lives.

"We had to do something that affirmed our heritage," Carl told me in a conversation one afternoon. "We had to find a way to uphold both the principle and the power of nonviolence. It seems so simple now, almost childlike innocence, but what we did was have signs printed up, small enough for people to put in their front windows but large enough to be legible from the street. 'This house is unarmed,' the signs said. It was my son Joel's idea. He was eleven at the time.

"They first appeared in only a few homes. But then a few more, and more after that. Soon people were making their own signs. And no house that had one saw any damage done to it or to the people living inside. In fact it was shortly after this that the tensions slowly began to ease. I don't know that we ended the revolt, but I do know that the courage of that witness gave people reason to pause and examine the ultimate futility of violence."

What are the things that make for a blessed peace? Courage, faith, discipline, love, maybe even a little ingenuity. And what do they yield? Rabbi Charles Sheer of Columbia University's Hillel Center, a thoughtful man of gentle temperament, described it to me this way: "There is an ancient prayer in the book of Numbers that describes for us the richness of shalom in our lives:

> The Lord bless you and keep you:
> The Lord make his face to shine upon you, and be gracious
>   to you.
> The Lord lift up his countenance upon you, and give you
>   peace.

"To bless and to keep," Sheer explained, "this is where it starts. It is a harkening back to the blessing of Abraham. A promise that God will provide, and that God will protect. From here is the promise of God's face shining upon us; a promise of illumination; of seeing the world as God sees it, in all its grandeur and majesty. Of seeing that despite the pain and suffering with which our world is imbued, there is still a triumphant beauty and goodness to it.

"Next is the experience of God's countenance, or, more specifically, God 'bestowing his favor,' by which we mean God looking kindly upon us, dealing gently with us, meting justice but tempering it with mercy.

"Providing for us, protecting us, instilling in us a sense of awe and optimism, looking upon us with mercy and forgiveness and expecting us to do the same," Sheer continued, "these are the things that make for a whole life. And so it is that when the blessing concludes with the word 'peace,' I believe we're meant to understand it as a punctuation, as the product of all that has preceded it."

Praying for Peace, Preparing for War

It would be grossly indulgent for us to translate peace into passivity, especially living as we do at a time when peace is under relentless assault from so many fronts, from terrorists masquerading as provocateurs against what they see as a corrupt status quo, to apologists of status quos who are themselves so corrupt as to be murderous.

The ancient Romans ruled over Jesus and his people with an edict called "Pax Romana"—the peace of Rome—but in fact it was not peace but subjugation by threat of death that kept the empire quiet. The "peace" they imposed on their empire was in reality quiet obedience under threat of punishment. Crucifixion is no small deterrent; it is the first-century equivalent of electrocution. Jerusalem, the very center of the holy land, is Hebrew for many things. But a place of peace it is not. It is a city that, since *before* the time of Christ, has known nothing but violence invoked in the name of God and quelled only by an occasional truce that is more often the product of fatigue than of principle. All wars before and since, anywhere in the world, be they declared or not, organized with faultless clarity or discharged in a moment's madness, the coordinated work of thousands of government employees with power and responsibility or the scheming of a renegade few with a rented truck or a highjacked plane, have been deadly testimony to the fact that our foundations of peace are not nearly as resilient as our penchants for war.

They are identified by names, these battles and wars. Names like Carthage and Waterloo, Dresden and Pearl Harbor, Dienbienphu and My Lai, Oklahoma City and Columbine; and however different one is from the next they are all hastened by a profoundly human inability to esteem the power of peace as a unifying force able to overcome all barriers by which we are otherwise divided. Instead they capitulate to the twin pillars of fear and pride. Said the apostle James, "you want something and do not have it, so you commit murder" (James 4:2), to which Paul adds: "For [God] is our peace; in his flesh he has made both groups into one and has broken down the dividing wall, that is, the hostility between us" (Ephesians 2:14).

I know of no issue more tragic than our unwillingness to live at peace with one another. Billions of dollars of resources that could go toward educating children (three hundred thousand of whom are currently fighting in wars throughout the world), conquering poverty, or curing diseases is diverted to waging the current war, preparing for the next one, or paying off the last one (and so it was in the days of Pax Romana that common people went hungry while the high ranking in the military class lived like royalty). Scientific minds best applied to the discovery of renewable energy sources are instead enlisted in the design of new and more insidious weaponry to protect oil reserves in far-off lands, where the international conglomerates that control them are neither understood nor particularly liked. We fight over boundaries and tribal rights, religious differences and ancestral feuds, ideological imperialism and hurt feelings. Sometimes, we don't even know why we fight, other than, as the Scriptures say, that "there is no peace in us."

If we learn anything from the peace that *is* in us it is that it represents the highest good to which not only persons but whole people can be called, and we cannot be content with our own serenity and at the same time indifferent to the swirls of anger that threaten to rend the fabric of society all around us. To do so would be to make of ourselves hypocrites, content to save ourselves and lose the world. We cannot believe in the mandate of a God who is eternally and universally loving and also believe it is a love that could be confined to a universe as narrow as our own horizons.

So it is that to be makers of peace we beat swords into ploughshares and spears into pruning hooks, missiles into mass transit systems and biological weapons into AIDS research. It is conversion of heart that leads the way for a conversion of communal and national priorities, from those that denigrate life to those that sanctify it. Or, as Marjorie Horton, a friend of mine and a stalwart member of Riverside Church's disarmament program, once put it, "You know, it seems to me the guy who builds the coffins can just as easily be making baby carriages. We were, after all, founded by a pacifist carpenter."

Contagious Peace

Be it a thing of the human heart or of the whole world, the uniquely personal quest for serenity or the relentlessly communal cry for what Malcolm X called "that brotherhood I so dearly want," peace comes when the enduring power and illimitable breadth of God's love is respected, trusted, and enacted. The peace of God is the shorthand of the Easter promise; it is a crucifixion that confers wholeness by promising us that even in those moments when sin threatens to tear us apart, God's love continues to hold us together, and it is a resurrection that confers comfort by promising us that that love will abide forever. Freedom from sin, freedom from death. The light in the jar. The light shines in the darkness, and the darkness has not overcome it.

Courage: Blessed Are the Persecuted for Righteousness' Sake

New opinions are always suspected, and usually opposed, without any other reason but because they are not already common.

—John Locke

Up to this point Jesus has extolled the value of a blessed life. Now, in an interpretation of Judges 5:31 that would be common among rabbis of both Jesus' time and ours, it is time he discloses its cost.

Jesus lived in a world that was unprepared for the radical breadth of his message, a world not unacquainted with these ancient teachings that he tried so hard to cast in a new light, but at the same time a world not ready, willing, or able to fully embrace them. Between the occupying forces whose job it was to maintain the status quo, the religious leaders who benefited from it, and the lowly poor and the peasants who despaired of ever changing it, his was an entrenched culture, wedded in a marriage of convenience to a litany of old conventions that served the few at the expense of the many.

Righteousness, as Jesus forewarned us a little earlier in the sermon, does not come easy. To be good with God can often mean to be at odds with society, friends, even family, and that's something that comes easily to no one. It means being true to the very core of who you are as a child of God, living in accordance with the dictates of a soul that has been enriched by faith and informed by conscience, which in turn means rubbing against the grain of someone or some group made uncomfortable by the extent to which those dictates countermand their own. It's easier to go unnoticed, to float with the tide. It's also safer, no crosscurrent to drown us in the skepticism of others. The righteous life is not the coward's life, but a life requiring enormous reserves of courage. It may not be a life for everyone, and of this fact Jesus intended to be quite clear. Many are called, few are chosen.

Clinging to the Known

But let us not be in too much of a hurry to condemn the reflexive conservatism of the first-century haves or the quotidian resignation of the have-nots, for it is in all of our natures—both as individuals and in community—to protect the familiar, regardless of whether that familiarity be a source of joy or an augury of destruction. For all the people who gathered on the mount so many years ago to hear what new message Jesus bore, many more stayed home that day because to them the unknown was like a deep sea in the dead of night—an alchemist's mixture that held both possibility and dread in its grip with equal force. Rather than cast themselves into the dark, they chose to stay huddled close to the realities—however burdensome—they had long since come to know.

> "God does not look you over for medals, degrees, or diplomas, but for scars."
> —Elbert Hubbard

I do not believe we've ever evolved beyond this ambivalent gravitation toward what we know over what we don't; I believe it is in our makeup to look upon the foreign and the unknown with a certain degree of caution, if not outright suspicion. I think, for instance, of Sally, a woman I once knew who was the victim of an abusive husband. Sally's was a miserable existence, and for a long time it showed no signs of getting any better. Despite the best efforts of those who cared about her, she chose to stay in this marriage because, in her words, "at least I know I can survive this. I don't know what the outside world would hold in store, and that frightens me even more." Only when her husband became increasingly arbitrary in his violence, only when *he* became as unpredictable as a future on her own, and her survival was no longer a thing she could guarantee, did she summon the courage to leave him and find her own way.

While Sally may be an extreme example, I believe by and large we all tilt our sails toward the winds we've ridden as opposed to those we haven't, to the accustomed as opposed to the exotic. We're traveling, say, in a foreign land, a place we have never been, where the culture and the topography, the customs and the language are unlike anything we've ever experienced. Somewhere along our journey we come upon two Americans, perhaps our age, perhaps from our hometown. We talk, swap stories of our adventures, maybe have a meal together. As rich an experience as this travel has been for any of us, we feel a relief and a comfort in having made this connection to our home. At journey's end, late one night when we have left the foreign place and returned to that home, we slip between the sheets of a bed we have long known and it holds us tight the way a mother's arms might. While the fresh memories of our trip will bring us twitches of excitement, the bed will bring us calm, and the sleep will feel good.

Like every other creature that returns to the nest or migrates each year to the same aerie or shore or spawning ground, it is within us to want to live within the boundaries of what we know, and for this reason it is sometimes difficult for us to greet the new and unknown without at least a hint of worry, even if it brings with it the promise of salvation. This is the warning Jesus was trying to sound for his audience: that they would meet with resistance from without *and* within, that a rocked boat seeks to settle itself, and that they would have to rely on their faith, their fortitude, their God, and one another for the strength that is necessary to lead what would literally be an eccentric (that is, "outside the prescribed circle") way of life.

The Risk of Eccentricity

It's not easy being different. I remember one evening some years ago, watching a performance of *Swan Lake* on television and having my two-year-old daughter, Kate, inspired by the production, begin banging around the living room in what in her mind's eye was surely the sylphlike movement of a seasoned ballerina. As she did so I could in my imagination almost hear the gentle strains of the great orchestra giving way to Nat King Cole singing, "dance, ballerina, dance. . . ." What was wonderful about that moment was that at Kate's age there is no such thing as a bad dance, no poor performance, no misstep; there is just the incalculable pleasure of free expression, the pure, ecstatic, unbridled joy of movement.

Only later, as she grew into the self-consciousness that begins to seep into a child's mind in her fifth or sixth year and never fully leaves, did she start to distinguish between good and bad in this way, and when she did, her dancing faded like the afternoon sun in a winter's sky, until eventually it pretty much disappeared over the horizon. Life had gotten darker, more complicated, and her dance was no longer as simple a thing as obedience to her inner impulse. It became instead the reserve of those who had the talent for it, those beautiful and graceful enough to slide this way and that across the ballroom floor as if on winged feet—only those lucky enough to be able to do it *right*. I was very sorry for this, but I believe I understood, and here's why.

Kate had reached an age—as all of us do—when she realized her actions, her looks, her very *self* were not simply experienced by others but evaluated by them. Behaviors are condoned and condemned by peer groups, focus groups, in-groups, out-groups. The rules of accommodation are written and rewritten to reward conformity and excellence, be it in style of dress, affiliation of friendships, mastery of skills, taste in television shows. Approval trumps freedom. You learn the rules, and then you play by them. My daughter's reluctance to dance, and so to risk the possible snickers and childhood persecutions of others, was something of a metaphor for me, for the price we pay when we dance outside the circle, and the pressure we feel to stay put within its defining, confining arc.

So it was, for instance, that in his day Vincent Van Gogh was roundly condemned for the bold strokes and thickened texture of his impressionist art, as was Johann Sebastian Bach for rewriting the rules on harmonization in classical music. George Gershwin had to win over a highly dubious audience with the notion that jazz had a place at such an august venue as Carnegie Hall (he did so with *Rhapsody in Blue*), and Branch Rickey with the notion that blacks had a place in major league baseball (he did so with Jackie Robinson). When change is pushed upon us, it is in our nature to push back, with equal vigor.

On a more everyday level, let's suppose a new family buys a home in an established neighborhood. The moving van arrives, and some neighbors stop what they're doing to peer over their fences. They do so largely out of curiosity, but also with a vague, unspoken hope. That hope is that the newcomers will not disrupt the tidy homogeneity that circumscribes their little block. No pink house paint, one thinks. No loud stereos, another. No rowdy teens, another. No Jews, another.

The circle represents safety, even if it sometimes also represents the stifling of creativity or the tolerance of injustice. Which is why what Jesus proclaimed, as did the prophets before and after him, is that God's world is bigger than this, that he did not simply create this or that corner of the universe, that his love is not confined to an inner circle of a select few, but that the whole world is our opportunity and our obligation, the place where we must live in such a way as to be fully realized as human beings, in sometimes uneasy alliance with one another. This king who loved the love-less, who washed their feet and raised their dead and taught their children and healed their wounds and forgave their sins, whose ministry was very much lived on the outer edge, has called us here, to the sacred responsibility of an eccentric life, and all the bless-ings and costs that that will entail. As it says in the book of Proverbs, better is a little with righteousness than great revenues without right (16:8).

Nothing to Lose but Their Chains

Persecution for righteousness' sake. It was a lot Jesus asked of those who chose to follow him, to conduct themselves in ways that might

at times take them outside the dictates of Roman authority or religious legalism, especially as they felt powerless, their lives shaped
by forces outside their control. At any given moment their occu-
piers might demand they pay tribute to Caesar, or their titular king
demand taxes to the local government. Arbitrary imprisonments
were not unheard of, nor was capital punishment for petty crimes.
Jesus' adherents were summarily persecuted by an economic system that oppressed the lowest class of its citizenry, a citizenry that
accepted the institution of slavery; and by a religious institution that
systematized oppression against women, including the risk of death
women took each time they labored to give birth to the next generation. It was a hard way. Rewards were scarce, burdens great.

But maybe in the end this made it easier for them. Having
already come to know persecution, suffering, the slings of injustice, the humiliation of being second-class citizens in a third-rate
nation, what did they have to lose? Maybe there were those who
knew enough about what it meant to be persecuted for no reason
other than that they were born on foreign soil or to low estate, those
for whom persecution *was* the known and so the risk of living a
life in contradiction to the rules of the game—rules that had never
really served them anyway—didn't scare them so much as provide
them the opportunity to consecrate their struggles. Live a life of
love in a love-starved world, they may have thought. Open ourselves to the risk of God. Be kind to enemies, patient with
strangers, gracious toward family, and generous with friends. In
this way perhaps, as this man is teaching us, God will permeate our
souls, and then, who knows? I'll cast my lot with faith, and with
the faithful, and together, as the poet Ovid wrote right around that
time, we will form a multitude.

This is why the poor and the discontented can be so frightening
to the great and the powerful: driven to extremes by extreme deprivation, they can become emboldened by their misery and, if the
oppressing class fails to break their will like the snap of a dry twig,
they will instead yield like a sapling bent by the wind, only to snap
back with a whiplike suddenness to stand in strong defiance to the
storm. Perhaps Karl Marx wasn't so far off when he spoke of class
struggle and the need for the downtrodden to challenge injustice

and its perpetrators. To live in accordance with the ethical teachings of Jesus, with the Beatitudes, the Sermon on the Mount, the accrued wisdom of thousands of years of Judaic thought distilled into this one precise prescription for radical faith, meant precisely this: abandoning the sclerotic, demeaning security that they paid for with such profound unhappiness, and choosing instead to live lives of love for which they might have to pay with their very lives. In that prescription I hear the words of William James: "it is only by risking our persons from one hour to another that we live at all. And often enough our faith beforehand in an uncertified result is the only thing that makes it true."

To be persecuted for righteousness' sake. To be true to themselves as children of God, to resist in spirit and in act every precept or edict—imposed upon them by rulers both religious and secular whose very job it was to defy defiance—that in any way contradicted that righteousness. To be free. In this one gesture of accepting persecution lies all the promise and peril of life in extreme obedience to the will of God. Jesus did know this, and his mission was nothing if not to ensure that others knew it too. Not everyone would follow him. Not everyone would go to the mount that day, and of those who did, some would think him mad while others would slip quietly away. But others still would take the challenge and live the risk. Over the course of two thousand years some have rejected the faith because it is intellectually untenable. Others have preferred that faith only uphold society's sameness. And there have been those whose entire lives are fashioned as a response to the radical message of the faith. These three responses, rejection, indifference, and courage, and the shades and nuances in between, continue to this day to be emblematic of the Christian odyssey, exemplifying the competing claims that such radical faith makes upon us.

Plus ça change . . .

Jesus was nothing if not an astute judge of human character; in blessing the persecuted he knew that he was addressing an audience wider than the one before him and a time both broader and more circumscribed than the culture in which they found themselves. To speak the truth where the truth is not welcomed is to travel the path of great resistance, a path counterintuitive to our inherent need to find approval in the eyes of others. To live a life that is right with God and honest to our essential selves is to scale a mountain no less steep today than it was two millennia ago.

Now the father of an early teen, I think of the enormous pressure children as young as nine or ten are subjected to these days to swallow a dose of designer drugs, throw back a shot of hard liquor at a friend's party, or smoke cigarettes for the cosmopolitan cool it pretends to. I think of the mysteries of sex being reduced to the status of conquest, and how much childhood innocence our kids can lose in the insistent drive to be older than they really are. They seem to know the codes of engagement; and resistance, never easy, only increases in difficulty as they get older. The rules of the dance become tighter, more constricting. They want to cling to the fabric of their own integrity, but it is hard for them when to do so means to risk rebuke and rejection from the very group they want so much to be part of. To be persecuted for righteousness' sake, for doing what they know in their hearts is right for them, can make for lonely times. It's a lot to ask anyone, let alone a young child, to stand alone in a right state. I have nothing but profound admiration for those who do, and as a testimony to the strength of our youth, there are many.

Righteousness is an exceedingly cumbersome thing because it means asking hard questions that others might not want to hear. I think of my years as a minister at a church that tried so hard to be socially responsible without being reckless, and the questions that tension generated for us. Why, a church member might have asked, are our trustees investing a portion of our portfolio in tobacco products? Or gun manufacturers? Why does our nation refuse to recognize the legitimacy of gay marriage, or our denomination the validity of gay clergy? Why have we not yet elected a Jew, or a woman, or an African American to the presidency of the United States, and what are we doing about it? What will happen to the rivers and streams we engorge with toxic waste, the forests we clear-cut for lumber, the wildlife refuges we pierce with oil wells, and what are we doing to protect our environment? Will the church be a critic of injustices or simply a mirror of the broader society that has cultivated them?

What makes questions like these even harder to hear in broader society is the knowledge that there are no easy answers. Righteousness interferes with the pursuit of our pleasures and the protection of our preconceptions. It can be expensive, inconvenient, and time consuming. It forces us to examine our priorities and assess whether and to what extent our actions take into account the needs, feelings, and rights of others. For these and other reasons it is met with persecution, resistance.

Some years ago I lived in a neighborhood in New York City where a social service agency was seeking permission to open up a halfway house for mentally ill young adults. I suspect if you polled us, one at a time, you'd find overwhelming support for a humane mental health system because in theory it's a hard thing for anyone with even a shred of conscience to fault. Nevertheless, most of us were loathe to see the house come to our neighborhood for fear that it would drive down property values, and the few who advocated for it—solely on the basis that it was the right thing to do—faced extraordinary resistance from the many who were more concerned about sheltering their investment than sheltering their emotionally needy brothers and sisters.

Similarly, some years later, when I was on staff at Riverside and the United States was preparing to go to war in the Persian Gulf, the church voted to grant sanctuary to any military personnel who had filed for conscientious objector's status but whose case the government refused to hear. Three young men risked imprisonment by accepting our offer, but the church itself became the target of anonymous threats for having given these men the right to try and plead their case that for reasons of conscience they should not be compelled to participate in what turned out to be an unnecessary but terribly popular war. Nevertheless, it was always a source of great pride to me that Riverside lived by the dictum that every church should live by: if you have no enemies in high places there is something terribly unpopular that you should be doing and aren't.

So whether it's children daring to listen to their hearts at the expense of their status among friends, advocates for a group of people who cannot advocate for themselves, or soldiers who demonstrate their courage by refusing to fight and kill, the world is rich with stories of brave souls who choose to bear the cost of discipleship and pay dearly for it while they wait for the rest of the world to catch up to them.

It is in this same vein that I think of the many heroes of the previous century who, during World War II, risked their lives to hide refugees in the cellars, attics, and secret rooms in their own homes so the refugees wouldn't be found and exterminated by the Nazis, or the Freedom Riders of the '60s who traveled far from *their* homes to help rid the south of its Jim Crow racism and prejudice. I think of the dulcet tones of the great Marian Anderson, who so generously let the Daughters of the American Revolution off the hook for denying her, a black woman, the right to sing in Washington D.C.'s Constitution Hall. "I forgave the DAR many years ago," she said. "You lose a lot of time hating people." And I think of people like Ben Spock, César Chávez, Jennifer Casolo, Sister Elizabeth MacCalister, and the Berrigan brothers, all of whom willingly, frequently, and even cheerfully exposed themselves to arrest and imprisonment for protesting unjust policies this country and other countries had no right adopting in the first place.

Beyond this I think of the innumerable everyday people we might run into in our grocery stores and Rotary Clubs, church suppers and synagogues, block associations and PTA meetings, all of whom, in their own subtle ways, go about the business of living as God would have them live, and quietly and without fanfare or complaint bear whatever price a life of principle might exact.

But to What End?

Contrary to the opinion of some cynics, the point of Christianity is not simply to withstand life and abide suffering but to embrace life and redeem suffering. As an old Baptist friend once lamented, "Sometimes I think people see religion as nothing more than the

Obedience to the Higher Cause

The story goes that the essayist Henry David Thoreau was imprisoned for protesting the institution of slavery. When fellow writer Ralph Waldo Emerson paid a visit to him, Emerson looked in at the cell and said to him, "What in the world are you doing in there?" to which Thoreau replied, "No, sir, the question is, what in the world are *you* doing out *there?*"

nagging fear that somewhere in the world, someone is having a good time."

Persecution for persecution's sake, the classic martyr's complex, is nothing more than glorified masochism with a dose of narcissism thrown in for good measure, self-mortification before a friendly audience. Suffering must mean something to be worth something. Rabbi Abraham Twerski tells the story of a man sentenced to years of hard labor, whose legs were shackled to a wall in his prison cell. Each day the man was forced to turn a heavy wheel, which he imagined was operating a mill that ground grain, or perhaps a pump that extruded water from the ground. At the end of his imprisonment, when the shackles were removed, he ran outside to see what good work his suffering was accomplishing. But when he got outside, he discovered the wheel was attached to nothing. His work was for no purpose. He collapsed under the weight of the absurdity of it all. *His suffering was not redemptive.*

This is not what God intends for us, though, and this is not what Jesus was getting at in this verse. Instead, I think he is saying that if the world is to be saved from its own devices it will be because there is a purchase for the price people pay. Small gestures attach to big dreams and do so in fits and starts, around small campfires and upper rooms, on dusty roads that lead to godforsaken places like Emmaus, or Samaria, or Johannesburg, South Africa, where struggles are engaged and, one day, overcome. It will happen because faithful fools, fools for Christ, as Paul called them, surrounded by indifference at best and hostility at worst, will follow their hearts. This world, Jesus is saying, this glorious, perilous world, is not yet ready for what it knows in its soul it desperately needs. It must be aroused to it, must be stirred, and like a great sleeping beast, it will resist. But, God willing, it will also one day relent, for as John Steinbeck wrote in *Sweet Thursday,* people "do change, and change comes like a little wind that ruffles the curtains at dawn, and it comes like the stealthy perfume of wildflowers hidden in the grass."

I think Jesus is flagging persecution more as an invitation than a warning. I think he's telling his audience that in order to put flesh on the bones of a fragile faith, people will have to band together, look after one another, and bind to one another with a love that is greater than the sum total of all the jealousies and resentments that might now keep them apart. You will have to become more than strangers on a mountainside, he is telling them, for in the days ahead you will need to become community, the living body of these living words.

This is the meaning of the "church invisible," an ancient appellation of the church in its purest essence. It is the *koinonia* community, a fellowship that has no regard for sectarianism or faction. It is the place for those whose persecution is the result of their faith, the test of their faith, and the strengthening of their faith; the coming together in faith *and doubt* of all good people—of any religious confession—who wish to evince a new creation and commit themselves, side by side, to making it happen. To creating a world where harvest bounties are shared equally among all people, where the dignity of work is affirmed by a decent paycheck, where colors that distinguish us don't divide us, where the pride of patriotism doesn't dissolve into the arrogance of nationalism, and where nature's beauty is revered rather than ravaged.

For Theirs Is the Kingdom

With this promise of redemptive suffering, of suffering for the sake of spiritual progress, Jesus brings the Beatitudes full circle; the kingdom that is promised in the first beatitude is fulfilled in the last. It is the breaking in of a new world upon an old one, the glacial change enacted by human beings as agents of the Almighty, that brings peace to a reluctant earth.

This is what we must be ready for, he is telling us, for change happens in this way: slowly, sometimes imperceptibly, and with great difficulty.

Think for example of people like Lucy Stone, a lone voice in the nineteenth century who heralded the right of American women to vote. It was only years later, when thousands of other voices had been added to hers, and marched, and prayed, and petitioned, that it came to be so. Lucy's righteousness, and her willingness to pay for it, made her country a little more right.

Or consider the photographs of Jacob Riis, a single man who set out to chronicle urban poverty armed with nothing more than a camera and an idea. Because of his exposé, a small group of citizens begins to question the morality of children working in factories instead of in schools; and, fighting an uphill battle against the men who own those factories, they whittle away at their resolve, make their case, gain a following.

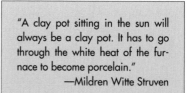

"A clay pot sitting in the sun will always be a clay pot. It has to go through the white heat of the furnace to become porcelain."
—Mildren Witte Struven

Long after Riis and his followers have left this earthly plain, the seeds of their efforts bear the sweet fruit of victory. Children will be educated, the society proclaims, not exploited.

More singularly, I think of a patient I once had who had lived a long and tortured life of alcohol abuse—his dirty little secret—for which both he and his family paid dearly. Then one day, tremulously, his daughter bettered fear with courage and dared to intervene, and put in motion what would be a years-long journey for that family toward some semblance of health, wholeness, and restoration. Steinbeck's wind, ruffling the curtains at dawn.

We have come some distance in the emergence of this kingdom, the leisurely blossoming of this vivid bouquet. And we have a long way to go, for we are still far from home. The obstacles are many, the roads steep and rutted, the persecutors plentiful, the demons Dionysian, tempting, and beautiful. The process is slow. But we will roll on together, each one of us, for we are the pebbles that compose a landslide. We will come down from that mountain, arm in arm, and we will not be fatigued. We will go with him to Jerusalem, and to all the Jerusalems, and we will not be deterred. We will go to Gethsemane, what Camus called our own private Gethsemane, and we will not be afraid. We will go to Calvary, and to all the Calvaries, and we will not let death have the final word. And we will go to the empty tomb, the ultimate triumph, and from there to the irresistible awakenings of a world turned upside down, the kingdom of God on earth.

Citation of Sources

Page 6   Abraham Joshua Heschel, *New York Journal American*, April 5, 1963
            Nadia Boulanger, *Mademoiselle*, Carcanet, quoted by Bruno Monsaingeon, 1985

CHAPTER 1: THE RABBI SHOWS US THE WAY OF THE KINGDOM

Page 17   Billy Graham, preface, *The Secret of Happiness*, W publishing, 1997
Page 23   Dag Hammarskjöld, *Markings*, Random House, 1966
Page 24   Søren Kierkegaard, *Works of Love*, Princeton University Press, 1998

CHAPTER 2: SURRENDER: BLESSED ARE THE POOR IN SPIRIT

Page 27   Mother Mary Madeleva, *My First Seventy Years*, Macmillan, 1959
Page 31   Henri Nouwen, lecture, Yale Divinity School, 1976
Page 31   Baba Ram Dass, lecture, Ann Arbor, Michigan, 1986
Page 33   Thomas Merton, *Conjectures of a Guilty Bystander*, Image Books, 1968
Page 34   Roger Rosenblatt, *Consuming Desires*, Shearwater Books, 1999
Page 35   Robert Heilbroner, prepared for Bread for the World and reprinted with author's permission
Page 37   Jack London, *Martin Eden*, Penguin, 1993

CHAPTER 3: EMPATHY: BLESSED ARE THOSE WHO MOURN

CHAPTER 4: PATIENCE: BLESSED ARE THE MEEK

CHAPTER 5: SELF-DENIAL: BLESSED ARE THOSE WHO
HUNGER AND THIRST AFTER RIGHTEOUSNESS

Page 69   Father Dennis Hamm, quoted by Rev. Gregory
             Sutterlin
Page 78   Alphonse de Lamartine, *Meditations Poétiques*,
             Lafayette Books, 1960
Page 80   Tennessee Williams, recalled on his death
Page 81   Lui Chi, *The Family of Man*, Museum of Modern Art,
             1996

CHAPTER 6: CONTRITION: BLESSED ARE THE MERCIFUL

Page 83   Ruth Smeltzer, quoted by Cyber-nation, www.cyber-
             nation.com
Page 86   Henri Nouwen, *With Open Hands*, Ballantine, 1972
Page 88   Studs Terkel, personal conversation, July, 2001
Page 90   Alan Watts, *The Wisdom of Insecurity*, Random
             House, 1968
Page 90   Simone Weil, quoted by Wendy Farley, *Tragic Vision
             and Divine Compassion: A Contemporary Theodicy*,
             Westminster/John Knox Press, 1990
Page 94   William Shakespeare, *The Merchant of Venice*
Page 95   John Steinbeck, *The Grapes of Wrath*, Penguin, 1992

CHAPTER 7: SANCTIFICATION: BLESSED ARE THE PURE
IN HEART

Page 97   August Wilson, interview, *The Baltimore Sun*, April
             23, 2000
Page 98   Malcolm Muggeridge, from *Something Wonderful for
             God*, documentary, BBC
Page 99   Annie Dillard, *For the Time Being*, Vintage, 1999
Page 100   George Zabelka, personal conversation, 1984
Page 101   See Shel Silverstein, *A Light in the Attic*, HarperCollins
             Juvenile Books, 1981

Page 103   T. S. Eliot, *Ash Wednesday*, Harcourt Brace, 1963
Page 104   Dennis Linn, et al., *Sleeping with Bread*, Paulist Press, 1994

CHAPTER 8: WHOLENESS: BLESSED ARE THE PEACEMAKERS

Page 109   Norman Cousins, *Saturday Review*, April 15, 1980
Page 109   Rabbi Hillel story as told by Rabbi Charles Sheer, June, 2001
Page 109   Rabbi Eugene Borowitz, from a poster for Argus Communications, 1969
Page 111   Emily Dickinson, *Complete Poems*, ed. Thomas Johnson, Little, Brown, 1960
Page 114   Thich Nhat Hanh, from a conversation at The Riverside Church in the City of New York, 1995
Page 114   Marcel Proust, *Remembrance of Things Past*, Knopf, 1982
Page 115   Hannah Arendt, *New Yorker*, September 12, 1970
Page 118   Carl Andreas, personal interview, August, 2001
Page 118   Rabbi Charles Sheer, personal interview, June, 2001

CHAPTER 9: COURAGE: BLESSED ARE THE PERSECUTED FOR RIGHTEOUSNESS' SAKE

Page 123   John Locke, *Essays Concerning Human Understanding*, E. P. Dutton, 1979
Page 124   Elbert Hubbard, *The Note Book*, Kessinger Publishing, 1998
Page 129   William James, *William James, Writings*, Library of America, 1992
Page 132   Marian Anderson, *New York Times*, December 13, 1963
Page 133   Rabbi Abraham Twerski, *Do Unto Others*, Andrews McMeel, 1997
Page 134   John Steinbeck, *Sweet Thursday*, Andre Deutsch, 1991
Page 135   Mildren Witte Struven, quoted by Jean Harris, *Stranger in Two Worlds*, Macmillan, 1986